DIY Project Based Learning for Math and Science

Are you interested in using Project Based Learning to revamp your lessons, but aren't sure how to get started? In *DIY Project Based Learning for Math and Science*, award-winning teacher and Edutopia blogger Heather Wolpert-Gawron makes it fun and easy! Project Based Learning (PBL) encourages students and teachers alike to abandon their dusty textbooks and instead embrace a form of curriculum design focused on student engagement, innovation, and creative problem solving. A leading name in this field, Heather Wolpert-Gawron shares some of her most popular units for Math and Science in this exciting new collection. This book is an essential resource for teachers looking to:

- create their own Project Based Learning units;
- engage students in their education by grounding lessons in real-world problems and encouraging them to develop creative solutions;
- incorporate role-playing into everyday learning;
- develop real-world lessons to get students to understand the life-long relevance of what they are learning;
- assess multiple skills and subject areas in an integrated way;
- collaborate with teachers across subject areas;
- test authentic skills and set authentic goals for their students to grow as individuals.

Part I of the book features five full units, complete with student samples, targeted rubrics, a checklist to keep students on track, and even "Homework Hints." Part II is a mix-and-match section of tools you can use to create your own PBL-aligned lessons. The tools are available as eResources on our website, www.routledge.com/9781138891609, so you can print and use them in your classroom immediately.

Heather Wolpert-Gawron is an award-winning middle school teacher and a popular blogger through Tweenteacher.com and Edutopia.org. She is also author of *DIY Project Based Learning for ELA and History*, as well as two other books with Routledge Eye on Education.

Other Eye on Education Books
Available from Routledge
(www.routledge.com/eyeoneducation)

DIY Project Based Learning for ELA and History
Heather Wolpert-Gawron

Writing Behind Every Door: Teaching Common Core Writing in the Content Areas
Heather Wolpert-Gawron

'Tween Crayons and Curfews: Tips for Middle School Teachers
Heather Wolpert-Gawron

Rebuilding Research Writing: Strategies for Sparking Informational Inquiry
Nanci Werner-Burke, Karin Knaus, and Amy Helt DeCamp

Beyond the Classroom: Collaborating with Colleagues and Parents to Build Core Literacy
Nanci Werner-Burke, Editor

**Teaching the Common Core Speaking and Listening Standards:
Strategies and Digital Tools**
Kristen Swanson

Authentic Learning Experiences: A Real-World Approach to Project-Based Learning
Dayna Laur

**The Classes They Remember: Using Role Plays and Mock Trials to Bring Social Studies and
English to Life**
David Sherrin

**Teaching with Text-Based Questions: Helping Students Analyze Nonfiction and
Visual Texts**
Kevin Thomas Smith

Common Core in the Content Areas: Balancing Content and Literacy
Jessica Bennett

**The Mathematics Coaching Handbook, Second Edition: Working with K–8 Teachers to
Improve Instruction**
Pia Hansen

**Creating a Language-Rich Math Class: Strategies and Activities for Building a
Conceptual Understanding**
Sandra L. Atkins

DIY Project Based Learning for Math and Science

Heather Wolpert-Gawron

Routledge
Taylor & Francis Group

NEW YORK AND LONDON

First published 2016
by Routledge
711 Third Avenue, New York, NY 10017

and by Routledge
2 Park Square, Milton Park, Abingdon, Oxon, OX14 4RN

Routledge is an imprint of the Taylor & Francis Group, an informa business

Library of Congress Cataloging-in-Publication Data
A catalog record has been requested.

ISBN: 978-1-138-89159-3 (hbk)
ISBN: 978-1-138-89160-9 (pbk)
ISBN: 978-1-315-70959-8 (ebk)

Typeset in Palatino
by Apex CoVantage, LLC

Printed and bound in the United States of America
By Edwards Brothers Malloy on sustainably sourced paper.

To Royce,
I dedicated the last book to our boys, and now it's your turn.
Life with you is like living the 4Cs: Collaboration, Creativity, Critical Thinking,
and Communication. Our life is one big PBL unit; we're learning together every day,
and I love every lesson and activity as we share this adventure together.

Contents

eResources ix

Meet the Author x

Foreword by Suzie Boss xi

Introduction 1

Project Based Learning, the Common Core, and the 4Cs 2

Experts Weigh In 4

A Teacher's Maker Movement 6

How to Create Your Own PBL Unit Focusing on Math or Science 7

How This Book Is Different Than Other PBL Books 10

Part I: PBL Lessons 13

1   **The Genius Unit:** A Unit Based on Informational Reading and Scientific Lab Reports 15

Overview 15

Step-by-Step Lessons 16

Tip on How to Assess Writing Quickly #1 24

Student Exemplars 25

2   **The Invention Unit:** A Unit Based on Inventing Solutions to Common,
Everyday Problems Using Persuasive Pitch Writing, Crowdsourcing,
3D Printing, and Digital Commercial Production 33

Overview 33

Step-by-Step Lessons 34

Tip on How to Assess Writing Quickly #2 49

Student Exemplars 49

3   **The Galapagos Unit:** A Unit Committed to Funding a Mission to Save
the Endangered and Unique Species of the Galapagos Islands Based on
Student Research, Role-Playing, Writing an Executive Summary of
Recommendations, and an Oral Pitch to the "Board" of a Major Institute 55

Overview 55

Step-by-Step Lessons 56

Tip on How to Assess Writing Quickly #3 67

Student Exemplars 68

4   **The Theme Park Unit:** A Unit Based on the Engineering of Building a Theme
Park Focused on Mathematical Trial and Error and Various Thematic Genres 71

Overview 71

Step-by-Step Lessons 72

Tip on How to Assess Writing Quickly #4 84
Student Exemplars 85

5   **The Teach Them to Be Teachers Unit:** A Unit Based on the Highest Level of
    Communication of All . . . the Ability to Teach 89
    Overview 89
    Step-by-Step Lessons 91
    Tip on How to Assess Writing Quickly #5 106
    Student Exemplars 106

Part II: Mix-and-Match Lessons to Design Your Own PBL Units 113
    Google Advanced Search. 115
    Six Steps of Being an Internet Detective 116
    How to Write a Newspaper Article 118
    The Problem Statement 119
    Writing with Numeracy Lesson 120
    Collaboration Constitution Assignment 123
    How to Comment on a Blog 124
    Online Ethics and Copyright Activity. 125
    Understanding Infographics Lesson 126
    Executive Summary Outline. 127
    Oral Presentation Timing Sheet 128
    Norms for Backchanneling and Using Twitter. 129
    Internet Literacy: Verifying the Evidence Lesson 130
    Cornell Notes 131
    Oral Presentation Rubric. 132
    Business Letter Outline 133
    How to Conduct an Interview 134
    QRF (Question-Response Format). 135
    Oral Conference Feedback Sheet 136
    Norms for Video Conferencing 137
    Developing a Student-Created Assessment 138
    How to Annotate Text 140
    Visual Presentation (PowerPoint) Guidelines 141
    Advocacy/Argument Outline 142

    References 143

eResources

The mix-and-match lesson materials in the book are also available as free eResources on our website so you can easily print and copy them for classroom use.

Go to the book's product page, www.routledge.com/books/details/ 9781138891609, and then click on the tab that says eResources. They will begin downloading to your computer.

Meet the Author

Heather Wolpert-Gawron is an award-winning middle school teacher who also writes a popular education blog as Tweenteacher. She has authored a number of series of workbooks: Internet Literacy for grades 3–8, Project Based Writing for grades 3–8, and Nonfiction Reading Strategies for the Common Core for grades 1–7. She is also the author of *Writing Behind Every Door: Teaching Common Core Writing Across the Content Areas* and *'Tween Crayons and Curfews: Tips for Middle School Teachers*, both written for Routledge/Eye on Education Publishing.

Heather is a staff blogger for the George Lucas Educational Foundation's Edutopia.org. She is a fellow of the National Writing Project and is devoted to helping teachers regain control of their profession through elevating their practice and educating themselves on policy. She is passionate about educational technology and blended learning, and she works to help tech-tentative teachers become more savvy online and off.

Heather is dedicated to a new educative movement, one that casts teachers in the roles of curriculum designers and archivists. She believes teachers have a vital role to play in K–12 instructional design.

She is wife to Royce, whom she met in second grade after karate chopping him at recess. Additionally, she is mom to eight-year-old Benjamin and three-year-old Samwise (yes, like the Hobbit), whom they call Sam. She lives with all her boys and their boxer/corgy mix, their laughter and chaos, in Los Angeles, California.

Foreword

Suzie Boss

So, a guy walks into an elevator and asks, "What the heck *is* Project Based Learning anyway?"

Unbelievable? Not if the storyteller is Heather Wolpert-Gawron. This inspiring educator is on a mission to make learning meaningful, motivating, and enjoyable for students and teachers alike. PBL is her method. In the classroom, she leverages everything in her toolkit, from anecdotes to authentic assessment strategies, to cause her students "to feel something, sensing in themselves their own growth."

With her *DIY Project Based Learning* books, Heather opens up that extensive toolkit and invites fellow teachers to take a look—and borrow liberally. It's a generous move by a teacher who has worked hard to develop her own deep understanding of PBL and to design projects that resonate with students.

From working with teachers interested in PBL myself, I know that newcomers to this instructional approach benefit from examples. Few of us, after all, had a chance to learn this way when we were students. Some teachers struggle to imagine how they can guide students through engaging project experiences and also meet serious learning goals.

Heather paints a vivid picture. As she describes her creative process for designing academically rigorous projects, I can imagine sharing a table with her at her favorite tea shop and talking through project ideas together.

The projects Heather brings into her middle school classroom align with Common Core State Standards. But that's not where her design process begins. As she explains, "Frankly, I'm selfish. I prefer to enjoy what I'm doing. I want to be excited about what I'm about to present to the kids. That way, my excitement trickles down to my students. Working with the standards at the forefront of my mind and the content in the background is a stinky model. I prefer to flip that way of thinking." She recommends designing "towards what you love. Think about your own interests and the interests of your students." From there, it's a matter of looking at the standards and finding a good fit.

Heather deconstructs several of her classroom-tested projects to show how PBL unfolds, from start to finish. She gets into the nitty-gritty, with specific details about the teaching strategies and learning activities she incorporates into each project to build students' mastery of concepts. She shares the tools that help her students manage their time, along with the digital tools she integrates to take learning deeper. Want to learn how to leverage a Twitter backchannel or do a collaborative writing activity using Google Docs? She shows how it's done. For anyone curious about the outcomes of PBL, Heather also offers samples of student work.

There's more advice here on everything from how to assign homework to how to plan authentic assessment. The second half of the book is packed with templates and tools just waiting for you to borrow and incorporate in your next project.

Along with the excellent advice she packs into these pages, Heather infuses her writing with personality, humor, and reflection. She shows by example why teachers shouldn't hesitate to bring their passion and humor into the classroom. She also makes a convincing case for collaborating with colleagues to expand PBL possibilities.

Many teachers find their way to PBL out of a desire to give students more voice and choice in their education. What does that mean in practice? For starters, Heather recommends being transparent with students about the big picture of any project. Let students know what's coming up, including the assessment plan. She also reminds us of the value of peer-to-peer learning. As she explains, "Students must be taught how to teach. They must learn to teach each other, and in so doing, will learn to teach themselves. After all, education's job is not to always be there for the student, but to give them the skills to be their own source of education during their life."

What do students have to say about this approach to learning? Here's one of my favorite comments, from a student named Daniel: "What I think engages a student most is interactions with real-life dilemmas and an opportunity to learn how to solve them . . . Something so interesting that you could never, ever forget."

PBL is still the exception in most classrooms. With Heather's inspiration and guidance, more students can look forward to taking part in unforgettable learning adventures.

Suzie Boss
Education Consultant and National Faculty Member
for the Buck Institute for Education Portland, Oregon

Introduction

When you first get into the swing of teaching, I mean, when you first really start feeling like you know what you're doing, your next step is to figure out what you really love about teaching. I'm not talking about why you do it. We all teach for many reasons: we love the students, we want to give back, we want to pass on a passion for a subject that we love, we want a reliable paycheck. All are great reasons to love teaching.

But it takes a while to get good enough at the science of teaching to then decide what you really love about it. For me, it's curriculum design. I love designing lessons and units that really connect with kids, that really help them learn to communicate, and that really leverage the love of learning in order to achieve. Many Saturdays, one can find me at the Chado Tearoom in Pasadena, California, laptop opened, clicking away, for hours at a time, devising some new unit of study for my students. The waitresses who know me are kind enough to seat me away from the main restaurant area and keep the tea and finger sandwiches coming until I rise from my dreamlike state of curriculum design. For me, designing curriculum is like writing a story, and I can get lost in it.

I'm like a student myself. Sometimes I write something that makes me laugh out loud, or sometimes I come across a resource that makes me cry, one that I can see in the hands of my middle schoolers, causing them to feel something, sensing in themselves their own growth, and hopefully instilling in them a desire to share and communicate that resource with others much like I want to share it with them.

When I was a new teacher, I found that many resources that were adopted in the classroom bored me to a different set of tears. I grew frustrated. I'd think: *how can I transfer a love of learning of what I'm teaching if I don't emotionally connect with the material?*

I didn't understand why math textbooks were just explanations, examples, and questions. Over and over again. Explanations, examples, and questions. I didn't understand why science textbooks were brief biographies of those who have changed our existence combined with equally brief definitions of their discovered properties and inventions and the assumption that we would just take the author's word for it that the law or property should not be taken for granted.

As a teacher, it made me mad.

Life is storytelling, and I always wondered why our lessons and units couldn't tell stories as well. Why couldn't a unit be a vehicle for lessons that have a sense of purpose? Why couldn't an assessment be more about the journey of learning than the snapshot-one-day-test to see what was learned? After all, much like becoming physically healthy, learning should be a slower process if it's going to be long lasting. A quick series of lessons followed by a test is, as is going on a crash diet and then quickly defaulting back to weight gain, sure to result in equally temporary learning.

So soon after I became a teacher, I found myself in my first tea shop, surrounded by the required textbooks, designing units that told stories. Stories about life, stories about achievement, stories about problem and solution.

I had stumbled on a passion for developing units submerged in Project Based Learning.

I found that there were others like me, other teachers who loved to tackle a wider and deeper methodology of teaching and learning. But few were actually designing these units themselves. I began field testing my units with other teachers, finding those that worked only for my students because of my own understanding of how to build the units and finding those that seemed to work in many classrooms, not just those in which I delivered the instructions.

This book represents some of my most popular units and the lessons that can be worked into any number of them. After all, one can pick up a book on Project Based Learning, but many of them out there are about the rationale of PBL, not the day-to-day implementation of it. This book, on the other hand, gives you both. And with access to the "why" and the "how," I hope my passion for curriculum design is one that will help transform your own classroom.

Project Based Learning, the Common Core, and the 4Cs

You know the hardest thing about teaching using PBL? Explaining it to someone. It seems to me that whenever I asked someone the definition of PBL, it was always so complicated a description that my eyes would begin to glaze over immediately. So to help you in your own musings, I've devised an elevator speech to help you clearly see what's it all about.

An elevator speech is a brief one- to two-sentence answer that you could give someone in the amount of time it takes to go from the first floor to the second floor in an apartment building. I like this visual, and I use it with my students, because getting to the point and encapsulating the gist of something is vital in today's speaking and writing-heavy world.

OK, so the elevator opens up, and a guy walks in and out of the blue asks you, "What the heck *is* Project Based Learning anyway?" I don't know why he would ask that, but for the purposes of this fantasy it seems that any Joe off the street is fascinated by your response.

You respond accordingly. "PBL is the act of learning through identifying a real world problem and developing its solution. Kids show what they learn as they journey through the unit, not just at the end."

"That's it?" the guy asks.

"Well, no," you reply. "There's more to it than that, but this is your floor and we're out of time." He gives you a brief nod of thanks and departs, leaving you to think of all the richness that this definition does not, in fact, impart.

After all, if we just look at that definition, it doesn't state certain trends in PBL. So now that it's just you (the reader) and I talking, let's bump up that definition so it more accurately captures the power of this learning strategy.

PBL is the *ongoing* act of learning *about different subjects simultaneously. This is achieved by guiding students to identify, through research,* a real-world problem, *local to global,* developing its solution *using evidence to support the claim, and offering the solution using a multimedia approach to presentation using skills based in a 21st-century set of tools.* Kids show what they learn as they journey through the unit, *interact with its lessons, collaborate with each other, and assess themselves and each other. They don't just take a test or produce a product* at the end *to show their learning.*

You realize that this definition, while closer to accurate than the previous version, would have caused his eyes to glaze over, and you decide that the earlier definition is by far the more efficient version, even as it shortchanges the awesomeness of the strategy.

Because PBL is awesome when it is implemented by teachers who buy into its methods. It is exciting to teach using PBL, and that excitement of yours, in turn, causes excitement in your clients, the students.

Nevertheless, it took me a while to tease myself away from the daily drudge of teaching with disconnected lessons. You know what I mean. I'm talking about the daily lessons that might teach a skill, and perhaps that skill fits within a unit based on a topic or a theme, but each lesson works independently and can function without being embraced in a unit that connects them all in a learning story.

But I grew bored, and I was concerned that my students would too.

Teaching using PBL is the difference between the atmosphere at Disneyland and the atmosphere at a Six Flags resort. No offense to Six Flags, but their décor needs some serious work. At Disneyland, you are submerged in the story of each ride from the time you enter the line. The walls, the ceiling, the ground on which you trod as you advance to the actual ride, all support the end result.

Teaching with PBL is much the same. It couches lessons in a tale, a tale about a problem that must be solved or an activity that must be developed. The learning happens along the way toward the presentation of the solution. Along the way, students are asked to do any of the following:

- question
- research
- write
- speak
- solve
- work together
- argue
- analyze
- advocate
- synthesize.

This list goes on and on. But when you think about the Common Core Standards and the 4Cs, it's clear that PBL hits them all, almost without thinking about it.

According to the Partnership for 21st Century Learning, the skills of tomorrow are as follows:

- questioning
- independent learning
- compromise
- summarizing
- sharing the air
- persuading
- goal setting
- collaboration
- communication
- problem solving
- decision making

- understanding bias
- leadership.

You can also categorize future skills by simply diving them up into the 4Cs—Collaboration, Communication, Critical Thinking, and Creativity—all of which are hit with any PBL unit.

Testing needs to move beyond simple multiple choice and into a more performance based assessment, as we are seeing in the Common Core tests around the country. PBL is, in a sense, an extended performance based assessment. One that is deeper and richer and, as a by-product, makes students more flexible and more aware of the alternative methods of communicating knowledge.

After all, using Project Based Learning isn't about writing a state report. It's about using what you know about the state you study and then creating your own state. It isn't about building a replica of the Washington Monument. It's about researching someone to honor, designing your own monument, and persuasively pitching a committee to build it.

Project Based Learning typically is grounded in the following elements:

- role-playing
- real world scenarios
- blended writing genres
- multiple reading genres
- authentic assessments
- authentic audiences
- real world expertise brought into the classroom
- units that assess multiple skills
- units that require research and comprehension of multiple subjects.

Allow me to personify for a moment: PBL cares about our mission to educate all. PBL never forgets that one of our main jobs is to prepare students for the predicted future. PBL knows that students are not standardized, that they don't learn in a standardized way, and that our clientele can't be assessed in a standardized manner if we are looking to foster innovation. PBL keeps its eye on the ball no matter the trendy standard or curriculum package du jour.

Experts Weigh In

In my own journey toward total Project Based Learning implementation, I met many along the way who feel as I do. In fact, it seems you can't click open your Smartfbrief without seeing some article or post that highlights different aspects of Project Based Learning.

Different people have different reasons for using PBL, but they all recognize its importance in developing problem solving and addressing the need to bring more of the real world into the classroom.

In A.J. Juliani's book, *Inquiry and Innovation* (Routledge, 2014), he focuses on modeling methods in the classroom that work in the business world as well (like Google's 20% creative time theory of productivity). He also goes into detail about predicting what the world might be like years from now when our students graduate into its clutches. He predicts that we will soon have:

> A workplace that is more individualized and personalized than ever before . . . We've seen the shift, as Fortune 500 companies have begun embracing strategies used in start-ups. Those startups like Google, Apple, and Microsoft were all founded by innovators who believe in the power of inquiry . . . Without inquiry there is little to no innovation. It's our job in education to free up time for innovation. It's our job to open their minds to new ideas. It's our job to prepare them for the present and future possibilities.

Juliani also questions the traditional model of education when he predicts that many future jobs will be more heuristic in nature. He explains that "an algorithmic task is one in which you follow a set of established instructions down a single pathway to one conclusion. A heuristic task involves trial and error and discovering the solution by yourself . . . Heuristic jobs involve creativity and doing something new often." Sounds like PBL to me.

Project Based Learning is also catching on in other organizations as well. Mike Kyle is a former CEO who left the entertainment and marketing industry to launch an after-school facility dedicated to his childhood passion for forensics. His speech and debate academy, Nova42, incorporates Project Based Learning in much of what they do. Unlike many after-school academies, Nova42 isn't just drill-and-kill, rows and rows of students working toward competition at the expense of the learning, as many private debate organizations can be. He says:

> When I am able to apply the lesson or exercise to a real world event (such as a job or college interview) the student becomes much more engaged and shows more focus than if I were to simply lecture the importance. We often use role-playing and real world adult mentors to make it even more powerful.

Then there are those who see the benefit of using PBL when studying through the lens of teacher quality as well. When asked about why teachers should play an integral part in creating these PBL units, Barnett Barry, a key author of *Teacherpreneurs* (Jossey-Bass, 2013) and CEO of the Center for Teaching Quality, explains that "research shows that when teachers are involved in project-based learning, their students score higher on complex measures of academic achievement. We also know that when teachers are more engaged in designing their own work students are more excited about schooling."

In fact, David Orphal, a gifted teacher and member of the Center of Teaching Quality, wrote about PBL in his 2014 EdWeek article, explaining that "nearly all of our work is project based, so I try as often as possible to give students an authentic audience for their work. This makes students far more enthusiastic and invested in the outcome of their project."

Tony Wagner, expert in residence at Harvard's Innovation Lab, reported in a blog for Mind-Shift in 2014 that "content knowledge has to be engaging to kids. If kids aren't motivated, you can pour content knowledge in their heads and it comes right out the other ear . . . Above all, they need to be creative problem solvers." He continues, "Students are learning many more real world skills, as well as content knowledge, through projects . . . They're doing work worth doing. They're doing work that's interesting, and engaging."

The most important experts of them all, of course, are the clients themselves. What do students think about learning through a Project Based Learning unit?

To answer that question, after teaching a PBL unit based on the TED conference model, I asked students to reflect on what worked and what didn't. Surveying the students makes them more aware of the process in which they learned. After all, when one is learning in an engaged way, sometimes the cogs in the machine are invisible to the driver. I wanted to make sure the unit was more transparent, so at the end, I reviewed the list of lessons and skills that we covered to make it all happen. This not only serves to embed the content more deeply, but what results from the review is an unveiling of sorts of the bones of the story we have told together.

So I asked students to share their thoughts on whether they felt they learned more using these methods. What they describe as to why it is vital to use PBL in the classroom, I believe, is more convincing than the statements from a room full of academic experts.

From the mouths of my middle schoolers from the spring of 2013:

Sofia: *"I believe that it all boils down to relationships. Not relationships from teacher to student or relationships from student to student, but rather relations between the text and the outside world. [PBL] . . . brought me to a greater thinking, a kind of thinking where I can relate the past to the present and how closely they are bonded together."*

Yvette: *"If you relate the topic to the students' lives, then it makes the concept easier to grasp."*

Jason: *"Students are most interested when the curriculum applies to more than just the textbook. The book is there—we can read a book. If we're given projects that expand into other subjects and make us think, it'll help us understand the information."*

Daniel: *"What I think engages a student most is interactions with real life dilemmas and an opportunity to learn how to solve them. Also, projects that are unique and one of a kind that other schools would never think of. Also something challenging and not easy, something to test your strengths as a student and stimulate your brain, so it becomes easier to deal with similar problems when you are grown up and have a job. Something so interesting that you could never, ever forget."*

Natalie: *"I like to explore beyond the range of what normal textbooks allow us to do through hands-on techniques such as Project Based Learning. Whenever I do a project, I always seem to remember the material better than if I just read the information straight out of a textbook."*

Kevin: *"I, myself, find a deeper connection when I'm able to see what I'm learning about eye to eye. It's more memorable and interesting to see all the contours and details of it all. To be able to understand and connect with the moment is what will make students three times more enthusiastic about learning beyond the black and white of the Times New Roman text."*

A Teacher's Maker Movement

We have all heard about the Maker Movement and the innovation and excitement students generate as a result of participating in a Maker-based unit. But what if teachers could be encouraged to participate in their own Maker Movements? What might that look like?

In the Maker Movement, students are asked to innovate, create, and problem solve. They are asked to design, write, present, and eventually produce a product. For a teacher, however, their "maker movement" is in curriculum design, and their product is an original unit. After all, in order for us to encourage valuable innovation in our students, teachers need the freedom to be innovative as well. Teachers need to be a part of curriculum creation. After all, enthusiasm for learning is trickle down.

The reality, unfortunately, is that teachers are rarely encouraged to actually "make" anything they teach. By denying teachers their chance to develop their own creativity in curriculum, we deny them the power of modeling enthusiasm for their content and the process of delivering that content. We also inadvertently cause a stagnation of imagination and critical thinking in the very troops closest to the students themselves and those tasked with bringing out those very traits in our clientele.

Nevertheless, there are talented creators out there, and they can do more than simply work the die-cut machine in the lounge. There are people out there secretly yearning to design their own standard-based units. They are itching for the opportunity to be creative. There are also those who simply don't know where to begin. To be innovative, sometimes teachers just need a little support and a few models to learn from.

That's where this book comes in.

This book is meant to help you do just that: innovate. It's meant to help you create your own units, be inspired by those provided, and enjoy teaching again.

There's a garden to design. There's a building to construct. There's a piece of land to protect. All of these interests can become teacher-created curriculum units.

How to Create Your Own PBL Unit Focusing on Math or Science

Call me bass-ackward, but I don't design projects around the Common Core Standards. I design projects based on what I believe are engaging topics that encourage my curriculum. Having said that, I don't neglect them either. In fact, by the end of my design process, I would say I've become rather intimate with the series of standards I'm trying to hit.

Project Based Learning is very different from just assigning projects. Assigning a project is a simple assessment. PBL, however, is the unit that encompasses all the lessons, all the explorations, the research, and the delivery of a solution the students are trying to present. Driven by an essential or guided question, a PBL unit may culminate in a "project" in order to be the vehicle of the information being presented, but the end result isn't the proof of the learning. What is accomplished on the journey, however, is. It's about the process, not the end project.

In fact, designing and developing a Project Based Learning outcome is its own process, and while I don't tend to invite the standards to the party first off, they do end up being the guest of honor.

Now, I have a two-pronged approach to designing PBL units or even developing the performance based assessments for my own district. The first way, of course, is to look at the standards and work through each, sometimes trying to fit a square peg in a round hole.

I prefer, however, a different way to design. I think about what I would enjoy first and then backplan from there.

Remember, some of what PBL can offer is enthusiasm for learning, and frankly, I'm selfish. I prefer to enjoy what I'm doing. I want to be excited about what I'm about to present to the kids. That way, my excitement trickles down to my students. Working with the standards at the forefront of my mind and the content in the background is a stinky model. I prefer to flip that way of thinking.

For instance, when I first began building my Genius Unit (see chapter 1), a unit based on developing a scientific lab report centered on the definition of genius that focuses student learning about metacognition and brain research, I didn't think at all about the Common Core Standards until my checklists and lessons were designed and in front of my face.

I knew I wanted my students to write lab reports. I knew I wanted them to watch TED speeches and read informational articles from different sources. I knew I wanted them to look at different text structures and scientific journals.

But once the unit had been created, I knew the next step was to see what standards my enthusiasm had hit all by itself. I developed a little checklist of Common Core Standards that I keep tacked up on my corkboard for just such moments.

Using that tool, I saw that, all on my own, I had hit key standards for both Science and even Writing.

But once done, I looked at the matrix of standards, and I looked at my lessons and student objectives, and I realized I hadn't naturally gravitated toward other standards. So I back-planned and put in other lessons that filled those gaps. What I started with, however, was my enthusiasm.

To summarize, it becomes a basic process made up of three steps:

1. Design toward what you love. Think about your own interests and the interests of the age group you teach.
2. Look back at the Common Core Standards.
3. Fill in the gaps.

Of course, it's not always possible to fill in every gap. After all, at least in secondary, you really are limited by time. So that's where cross-curricular planning comes in. Find someone to partner with who might share your interest in your unit. Or look toward what other subjects are doing at your grade level and see if their curriculum naturally fills the gaps in your own matrix.

After all, we have to remember that we aren't the only ones with our hands on those students during their school year. There are others who, combining forces with your efforts, can share the burden of hitting those standards.

It's vital we collaborate. It's vital we open our doors and utilize the strengths of a team of teachers per student. The Standards are broad and vast and deep, so much so that one teacher cannot possibly hit them all with the depth necessary for true learning and transfer.

That being said, I begin developing a unit by creating a checklist.

Developing and providing checklists speaks to college and career readiness in the Common Core. After all, organization, preparedness, goal setting, and the independent learning that comes from utilizing resources are all folded into the expectations of these new standards.

But they also hit 21st-century skills and strategies presented by such websites as the Institute of Museum and Library Services (www.imls.gov/about/21st_century_skills_list.aspx), which calls for the following:

Manage Projects (Productivity and Accountability)
◆ Set and meet goals, even in the face of obstacles and competing pressures.
◆ Prioritize, plan, and manage work to achieve the intended result.

Manage Goals and Time (Initiative and Self-Direction)
- ◆ Set goals with tangible and intangible success criteria.
- ◆ Balance tactical (short-term) and strategic (long-term) goals.
- ◆ Utilize time and manage workload efficiently.

It's about transparency, and the more information you grant to students, the better. After all, if we're working to let go of the authority in the room and create a classroom where students own their learning, then we have to let them in on the sequence of lessons and assessments ahead of time. There's no reason why students should be in the dark as to what I will expect and why. The mystery defeats achievement.

There are many reasons to use checklists.

- ◆ They make sense of the big picture of a particular unit.
- ◆ They help me plan ahead, forcing me to think about where I want to go and how.
- ◆ They communicate to parents what we are doing in the classroom so there aren't mixed messages coming home regarding the purpose or pacing of assignments.
- ◆ They provide students a resource to develop better time management skills by planning and prepping assignments in advance.

Some checklists I provide are fully filled out in advance and copied (or shared via Google Drive). Others allow for students to fill them in. We sit down at the top of a unit and spend a period going through what will be required. I find that students have more ownership when it's in their own writing or typing, so it's time well spent. I have even, on occasion, permitted students to set their own deadlines on their checklists. However, once it's filled in, it acts like a contract, and that student must meet the deadline specified.

When developing your own checklists, make sure you backplan. When do you want the final assessment/presentation to be? Enter that date first on your checklist. Then fill it in from there, making predictions about how long it might take for you and students to accomplish particular tasks.

I always include a cover sheet that informs all stakeholders (students, parents, and administration) of the intention of a particular unit. This also includes a contact email or phone number where I can be reached with questions.

The table itself should also have a few empty rows. This goes hand in hand with a front-loaded conversation you need to have with students about being flexible. I consider flexibility another 21st-century skill. After all, you can only predict so well. You must tell students that while these assignments reflect the overall goals and lessons planned at this time, you still have the right as their guide to cross an assignment off the list or add one if you discover a gap in the learning once the unit begins. It's your call, and it's an all-important lesson in being flexible.

It's like a contract. You promise to think ahead, not to wing it, and be transparent with your plans. They, on the other hand, promise to plan ahead. So, as a teacher, you don't need to get too compulsive about providing every beat of a unit ahead of time. Your goal is to grant them access to your thought process as it exists to the best of your knowledge at this time.

So, what do students think of checklists? Well, I asked them, and they said the following:

Joshua: *"Our checklists give us a visual list of what we have to do. For example, a checklist would be better than paragraph instructions because we have to draw out a list from a paragraph, whereas in a checklist, we can immediately see what we need to do and get straight to work."*

Destiny: *"I am a procrastinator, and having the kind of motivation to check something off is great for me to stay on track . . . It's like if you have 10 parts of your assignment, for every one you check off, it's like a small victory."*

Alyssa: *"Checklists let me know about big assessments that may come in the future and allow me to plan for them. Checklists also keep me organized and help me remember what I have due and when for long-term projects."*

Caitlin: *"The human mind can become forgetful, and checklists help keep track of many things and ease the pressure of remembering certain things . . . They help you avoid minor/major mistakes."*

I mention checklists because they are vital to the organization and structure of a PBL unit. For, as any teacher who uses PBL can tell you, it can get unstructured pretty darn fast if you don't have some kind of scaffolding holding the organization of the unit intact.

To fill in that checklist with lessons and informal and formal assessments requires pulling from a toolbox of activities. Think of this book as a kind of toolbox from which you can draw.

How This Book Is Different Than Other PBL Books

Many PBL books are about using it Someday, not Monday. This book is meant to give you rationale and enthusiasm, to be sure, but it's also meant to get you started right away.

As I have said in my previous book, *Writing Behind Every Door: Teaching Common Core Writing in the Content Areas*, "If it doesn't exist outside of school, then it isn't worthy enough to be taught within school." Project Based Learning focuses on this mantra, and this book will provide methods teachers can use to follow through with its promise.

You'll find that this book is made up of two parts. These two parts can be combined to form any number of different PBL units.

The first part of this book is full of complete units. They include:

1. overviews and descriptions of a whole unit and the goals and objectives;
2. FAQs about the unit—subjects that are integrated, skills used, etc.;
3. step-by-step and day-to-day guides toward implementing the unit, including simple scripts if necessary and handouts as needed;
4. student samples;
5. targeted rubrics as necessary.

I've also included something called "Homework Hints." Sometimes with PBL, teachers get a little lost in the most traditional of assignments—homework. Throughout this book, I've indicated opportunities to assign independent take-home assignments that can be used to fulfill this requirement if you need it.

In addition, I've included tips on how to quickly assess the writing that might be produced throughout the unit. Having the students write is unavoidable, but it's possible that in your focus on teaching math or science, you might have lost some ease in giving feedback or assessing writing. I've included some tricks to quickly accomplish this so you can both hold students accountable for their STEM content and the quality of how they communicate that content.

Each unit also contains a checklist or pacing guide of assignments to guide both you and your students through a particular unit. In *Dandelion Wine*, Ray Bradbury writes that the grandma's kitchen was warm, exciting, and full of "organized chaos." I like to think my classroom environment is also like that. Well, at least it's a positive spin on the piles of books, the stacks of papers, and the uneven bulletin boards that define my middle school classroom.

I've also included, along our PBL journey, a few tips to help quickly score the writing that might need to be produced, even in a STEM-based unit. After all, the students have to communicate content, and writing should be utilized in every classroom if we expect ability to transfer from school to the world beyond.

The second part of this book includes a whole stack of resources that can be inserted into existing units or combined to create new, exciting ones.

If you know your students need a brush up on something like researching online reliably, for instance, I've got a lesson for that. If you find you need your students to have access to a typical outline for writing an argument, something that ELA teaches, but you, a math or science teacher, doesn't, there's one in here as well.

This structure allows you to mix and match your lessons to meet the needs of your students. It also allows you to tweak what I've developed and make a PBL concoction all your own.

Incidentally, many of these lessons are stand-alone activities or resources, so feel free to use them outside the realm of PBL. However, I would recommend housing them within a PBL unit so they have a full impact on the learner.

I hope this book helps you learn through doing. Don't wait to invent a unit yourself; look to mine as a way in to PBL. Then, I challenge you to go out and tweak, revise, and create yourself. You won't regret it as a teacher, and you won't regret it as a learner either.

Part I

PBL Lessons

The Genius Unit

A Unit Based on Informational Reading and Scientific Lab Reports

Table 1.1 Genius Unit Facts

Subjects Integrated	Writing—scientific lab report
	Science—brain-based research focus
	Reading—informational
	Technology—hyperlinking, Google Drive
Skills Used	Collaboration
	Problem solving
	Creativity
	Communication
	Questioning
	Role-play
Duration	2 weeks
Driving Question	What defines genius?

Overview

This unit was one of the first ones I worked on that was meant to experiment with a more truncated length. As it turned out, it served more as an extended Performance Based Assessment, even while it borrows elements from traditional Project Based Learning. It seemed to me that the only way to be able to totally teach using PBL would be to create units that varied in length to fit into the requirements of the district and school. After all, one can't keep moving along a pacing guide that doesn't permit for the occasional test or assembly or drill. I needed a few units that were shorter modules of learning that still had the elements of any deep PBL unit. This doesn't have them all, but it hits on the following:

- ◆ subject matter integration
- ◆ role-playing
- ◆ authentic assessment

- ◆ blended learning
- ◆ outside expert.

The Genius Unit addressed this need. It also focused on brain research, something I wanted my students to begin to think about more earnestly.

The basic premise is that the students are role-playing as medical professionals. They have a young client/patient they have been seeing who is showing signs of being a genius. The students are given daily resources that represent everything from magazine articles to blog posts to the Mensa test in order to define genius, study the strengths and weaknesses of labeling, and learn more about the process of identifying a true genius. The students will be asked to take notes in various ways and modalities ranging from traditional dual-entry journals to creating their own assessments. In the end, as the culmination of the unit, the fledgling doctors must write a formal scientific lab report using what they learn in their resources and research in order to advise the patient's parent of possible next steps.

Step-by-Step Lessons

For units of this length, I don't necessarily provide a formal checklist, but I do give students an overview of the week(s) so that they can manage their time. I will provide them an agenda that would look something like this:

January 6–17

MONDAY
Practicing for the Performance Based Assessment
Quickwrite: What is genius?
Think Different ad
Forming new table groups

TUESDAY
Jigsaw genius resources
Reading articles/sharing out

WEDNESDAY
Shakespeare's contributions to our language

THURSDAY
Taking the Mensa test

FRIDAY
DUE BY BEGINNING OF CLASS: Blog Post Jigsaw Activity
Compiling week's notes

MONDAY
OFF

TUESDAY
Jigsaw genius resources
Reading articles/sharing out

WEDNESDAY
Viewing model lab reports

THURSDAY
Taking the Mensa test

FRIDAY
DUE BY BEGINNING OF CLASS: Blog Post Jigsaw Activity
Compiling week's notes

MONDAY
DUE: Final Draft of Genius Blog Post
Changing your IQ activity
Learning about specific geniuses

TUESDAY
Quickwrite on Steve Jobs quotes
Interviewing a subject matter expert
DUE BY END OF CLASS: IQ Quiz

WEDNESDAY
Writing with numeracy
Brainstorming, organizing, and pre-writing

THURSDAY
DUE: Take the Quizzes
Argument essay using resources

FRIDAY
Argument essay using resources
DUE BY END OF CLASS: Scientific Lab Report

Let me walk you through it step by step.

1 **Quickwrite: What Is Genius?** This initial quickwrite will be a jumping-off point for discussion about how one perceives intelligence. By the end of the unit, we'll loop back to this

quickwrite to see if perceptions and definitions have changed once research has been conducted. This could be done as a blog post. Kidblog.org is a great resource for setting up simple blog accounts for students even if your school hasn't bought into a huge LMS system.

Blogging and quickwriting address the requirement that all students must be writing in every classroom. For instance, we know that in the math standards, students must justify and explain via writing. This can feel very inorganic unless writing is more deeply integrated into the curriculum. If a student is being asked to hit the following standard, for instance . . .

Understand solving equations as a process of reasoning and explain the reasoning.

CCSS.MATH.CONTENT.HSA.REI.A.1
Explain each step in solving a simple equation as following from the equality of numbers asserted at the previous step, starting from the assumption that the original equation has a solution. Construct a viable argument to justify a solution method.

. . . that requirement to "explain" would be much easier for students who have already been writing through a more scientific lens than for those who are only asked to "explain" when being assessed. Encourage all forms of writing and the assessment writing will be easier to construct.

2 **Think Different Ad:** This ad serves as an entry-level event: a launching pad for the learning to come that sets the tone of the unit overall. This one is narrated by Richard Dreyfuss, but there is another one narrated by Steve Jobs himself: www.youtube.com/watch?v=n-mwXdGm89Tk

This video not only aides as a discussion starter, but serves as a guide for further research that can help a student as he or she progresses through this unit. You can have students research each of the "geniuses" shown in the video or put students in groups to share the task of discovering the contributions each subject gave to his or her society.

3 **Jigsaw #1:** This unit scaffolds the learning from multiple resources by using the traditional jigsaw activity as a means to learn more thorough collaboration. In a traditional jigsaw, a small group of students might chunk an article so that each student becomes an expert at, say, one paragraph or one column or one page. They then share out what they've learned with the other students who, in turn, also share out the section assigned to them.

In these activities, students are divided into groups of four, and each student must become an expert at a different resource. Then, using Google Drive, the students must summarize their resource and share their notes with the students in their table group. See the following for the full assignment:

Jigsaw #1

In your table group, divide up the following resources. Each person should read the article assigned to them and become an expert on its contents. Then, using a Google Document, write a summary of your article, including the title of the article, website/periodical, and author. Identify the main point and include at least 2 important quotes. You must also end your document with 3–5 questions inspired by your assigned article. You can use both proper paragraph structure *and* more interesting text formats in order to convey the information in your article to your table fellows. Please use proper APA or MLA bibliographic formatting to cite your article at the bottom of your page.

Share your document with those at your table *and* with your teacher. Give us all the ability to comment.

Here are your resources:

Person #1. *Time*, Is Genius Born or Can It Be Learned? http://content.time.com/time/health/article/0,8599,1879593,00.html

Person #2. *Creativity Post*, How Geniuses Think www.creativitypost.com/create/how_geniuses_think

Person #3. *BBC*, Tell-Tale Signs of a Genius Child www.bbc.co.uk/news/uk-england-hampshire-1770V2465

Person #4. *Psychology Today*, The Downside of Genius www.psychologytoday.com/blog/innovation-generation/201307/the-downside-genius

A student sample of this activity can be found at the end of this chapter.

4 **Student-Created Assessments:** In my last book, *'Tween Crayons and Curfews: Tips for Middle School Teachers*, I wrote about the power of students showing their comprehension, not by taking tests, but by developing them.

Teach students about Costa's Levels of Questioning. These are simpler than Bloom's Levels. Teach them that there are three levels of questions. Level 1 asks your brain to work the least: recall a fact, define a word, etc. Level 2 bumps it up a notch. You might be asked to sequence or categorize some topics. You also might be asked to infer. The brain, therefore, is working a little harder. Level 3, however, is where the brain really begins to sweat. It asks students to create or predict or hypothesize based on what they know about the topic.

Next, teach students about the choices of formats in developing questions:

- ◆ multiple choice
- ◆ rank order
- ◆ true-false
- ◆ short-answer essay
- ◆ matching
- ◆ etc.

Have them then develop an assessment of 10 questions that mix and match levels of questions with formats of questions. These questions then become the basis of a more formal assessment.

More details on guiding students through inquiry and question development can be found in my "Teach the Teacher" unit in chapter 5.

5 **Jigsaw #2:** The next jigsaw activity focuses on a different set of resources. Each of these honed in on the concept of brain plasticity. For many students, this was the first time they had ever heard the term or thought about the fact that their intelligence wasn't static. The study that intelligence is actually dynamic and changeable is a powerful concept for many tweens and teens, many of whom, by the time they reach middle school, already feel their path has been laid in concrete.

However, while each student needs to still be responsible for learning his or her resource, the way the students are sharing their expertise is by creating a short, multi-level quiz. This quiz will be sent to each of the students in the table group, and each student must answer the questions sent to them by exploring the resources themselves at home. An example of a student-created assessment/quiz can be found at the end of this chapter.

Jigsaw #2

Assign each person in your group an article to read about the plasticity of our brains. Each one talks a bit on how fluid our IQ can be. When thinking about genius, the question has to be asked: can genius be learned?

Once you have read your article, you will then create a 10-question quiz using Google Forms. Your teacher will instruct you on how to create a quiz, customize it, etc. Think about levels of questions. How can you create a quiz that isn't all short answer essay while still using higher level questioning and inquiry?

Make sure you have the following structures in your quiz so your recipients don't get too bored:

◆ Multiple choice (one answer only)
◆ Short answer
◆ Checkboxes
◆ Scale.

When your quiz is completed, send it to your table group.
You must have your quiz completed by the end of class on Tuesday. You must complete all 3 quizzes sent to you by Thursday, January 16.

Person #1. *LiveScience*, 5 Experts Answer: Can Your IQ Change? www.livescience. com/36143-iq-change-time.html
Person #2. *Mental Health Daily*, 11 Ways To Increase Your IQ Score (Intelligence Quotient) http://mentalhealthdaily.com/2013/04/24/11-ways-to-increase-your-iq-score-intelligence-quotient/
Person #3. *Psychology Today*, Improving Intelligence www.psychologytoday. com/blog/exploring-intelligence/201302/improving-intelligence
Person #4. *Discovery*, Myths about Intelligence http://dsc.discovery.com/tv-shows/curiosity/topicsT/myths-about-intelligence.htm

---

Homework Hint

Have the students read their resources and develop their assessments during class. This way, they have access to you and you can ask them to share their quizzes for quick feedback and U-turns if necessary. Taking the quizzes, however, doesn't need to happen at school. Students can be asked to take their peers' assessments over the course of a week leading up to the final assessment.

6 **Jigsaw #3:** Although I try to devise different methods in which students can interact with texts, I looped again with this third activity to repeat the directions once more during this unit. I wanted the acts of summarizing, questioning, citing, and sharing to become second nature. This only happens through some kind of repetition.

Jigsaw #3 is the next assignment in this unit.

Jigsaw #3

As we did in Tuesday's class, we are going to do another jigsaw activity to work with multiple resources. You will become an expert at your article and then *share* it with your teacher and those at your table group. Write a summary of your article, including the title of the article, website/periodical, and author. Identify the main point and include at least 2 important quotes. You must also end your document with 3–5 questions inspired by your assigned article. You can use both proper paragraph structure *and* more interesting text formats in order to convey the information in your article to your table fellows. Please use proper APA or MLA bibliographic format to cite your article at the bottom of your page.

This activity is due at the **START** of class on Friday, and classmates will be commenting and compiling notes during class on Friday.

Person #1 (can't have read resource #4 from Tuesday's class). *Mental Floss*, 11 Historical Geniuses and Their Possible Mental Disorders http://mentalfloss.com/article/12500/11-historical-geniuses-and-their-possible-mental-disorders

Person #2 (can't have read resource #4 from Tuesday's class). *LiveScience*, The Connection between Genius and Madness www.livescience.com/20713-genius-madness-connected.html

Person #3. *McArthur Foundation*, McArthur Foundation Fellows for 2013 www.macfound.org/

Person #4. *Discovery*, 26 Genius Pictures http://dsc.discovery.com/tv-shows/curiosity/topics/geniuses-pictures.htm

---

Homework Hint

Have the students take the Mensa test at home. It isn't anything formal, and genius cannot be determined by its results, but it gives the students another format of information delivery from which to infer. They can think about the questions and use what they learn from the process to help them eventually create their own definitions of genius. The Mensa test can be found at www.mensa.org/workout.

---

7 **Compiling Notes:** It's important to handhold students a bit when it comes to note taking. Note taking is its own skill, and it doesn't come inherently to many people, much less students. What they need to know is that much of what they have been doing already is, in fact, a version of note taking. Building Cornell Notes (see Part II of this book) uses the skills of summarizing, questioning, and deriving the main idea, as do the assignments the students have conducted already. Now, it's just time to compile them all so they may access their content efficiently in time for the culminating report deadline.

For this next assignment, Note Compiling Activity, I've given students directives that might help them do just that.

Note Compiling Activity

OK, tomorrow you will begin constructing your culminating report. The actual writing will last for 2 days. You MUST submit your response by the end of class on Friday or it will be marked late on a test.

To help you out, I've created another note taking resource so you can compile your research in yet another way. I've also included a few other resources that I didn't fit into your jigsaw activities but that seemed relevant to the topic. Here they are:

Yahoo, 30 Intelligent Celebrities
http://finance.yahoo.com/news/the-30-smartest-celebrities-in-holly-wood-175417855.html
PBS, Multiple Intelligences
www.pbs.org/wnet/gperf/education/ed_mi_overview.html
Edutopia, Habits of Mind
www.edutopia.org/blog/habits-of-mind-terrell-heick
Scientific American, You Can Increase Your Intelligence
http://blogs.scientificamerican.com/guest-blog/2011/03/07/you-can-increase-your-intelligence-5-ways-to-maximize-your-cognitive-potential/

After skimming through those resources just so you know what you have access to for this activity, please respond to the following prompts:

1. What is genius? To respond, you do not need to answer this question again as you did in your blog post. Instead, list 3 quotes from any of this week's or last week's resources that answer it for you. They can all contribute something similar, or they can give varied definitions. Remember to cite where they came from so you don't have to search for that information during your writing days.
2. Name 10 known geniuses from our resources and hyperlink each name to an external website as a reliable resource.
3. Give a bulleted list of at least 5 drawbacks of being labeled a genius. These can come from yourself and/or your resources.
4. How does multiple intelligences relate to the concept of genius? Please use proper QRF format (Question-Response Format, see Part II of this book) and hyperlinks within your paragraph to respond.
5. Provide a works cited of articles read (copy and paste the bibliographical information of the articles you found the most interesting and may want to pull from for your upcoming assessment).

6. Develop questions compiled after each resource read (these can be yours or those developed by a different student).

7. Think on the following questions. Then copy the URL of related articles underneath each question to indicate the resource from which you may pull quotes if you were to synthesize a response:

What are the drawbacks of genius?

Does a genius have a responsibility to create something for the world?

Do you have to create something to be labeled a genius?

Is genius born or learned?

What is the difference between genius and intelligence? Is there a difference?

Homework Hint

Using the resources you have read or discussed this week, revise your Monday blog post on how you define "genius." Allow others to comment.

8 **Bring in a Subject Matter Expert:** For the purposes of this unit, you can bring in almost any medical professional as a face-to-face guest speaker or as a Skyped-in speaker. For norms on video conferencing in the classroom, see Part II of this book.

9 **Scientific Lab Report:** For the final assessment, the student will be asked to role-play as a medical professional and write a scientific lab report. It's important that we teach students that there are different genres of writing that can be specific to different careers. The world is not just divided into narrative, argument, analysis, and summary, as school seems to indicate. Of course, genres blend and incorporate elements from each other, but that's the result you want students to realize once they have explored different formats.

The first thing to do is to have students see model texts of actual lab reports. These primary documents can be donated by actual offices, or examples can be found online. This brings more authentic, career-based writing into the classroom in order to address our new requirements toward real world application in education.

10 **Writing with Numeracy:** This is meant to help students embed numbers correctly into their writing. You can learn more about this lesson in my Invention Unit, and this lesson can be found in Part II's mix-and-match section.

11 **Sharing More Resources for Note Taking:** If you feel students need more practice on note taking or informational reading, have them tackle any of the following additional resources. This list can continue growing as they themselves find resources to help them seed facts into their eventual lab reports.

Atlantic, Secrets of the Creative Brain
   www.theatlantic.com/features/archive/2014/06/secrets-of-the-creative-brain/372299/
ERIC Digests, The Pros and Cons of Labeling a Student as Gifted
   www.ericdigests.org/2004–2/gifted.html
Edutopia, Debunking the Myths about Gifted Students
   www.edutopia.org/blog/debunking-myths-about-gifted-students-heather-wolpert-gawron

12 **The Assessment:** The following is the actual prompt used in the final assessment in this experimentally short PBL unit.

You are a doctor who has been seeing a patient for some time. It has become apparent to you that this person (it can be a child or an adult) has outstanding characteristics in one field or another. You are slowly coming to the realization that this person may be characterized as a genius.

Write a lab report (see example) that informs the patient (or, in the case of a child, it should be his or her parents) that he or she may be a genius. You must cite evidence and research so it isn't just about your observations. You must also be gentle in your written voice because, after all, you must be straightforward with your patient(s). Your audience is both the family and for record keeping at your medical facility. In other words, you need to be informational. If you have a section that recommends something, then use some kind of persuasive techniques in your writing, but for the most part, you are writing as a professional.

Use the lab format as well as you can, but know that I am not grading on perfect scientific lab report formatting. Just let it give you some ideas of headings and how to organize your thoughts on the topic. You are also welcome to look through images online or other resources for formatting inspiration.

Remember, at this point, I am looking for voice, alternative text formats, writing with numeracy, hyperlinks, high-level writing, and an understanding of audience. Your written piece is due at the end of class on **Friday, January 17.**

 Tip on How to Assess Writing Quickly #1

Only focus feedback on one skill. Be selective in what you want to see from the students. If you want to make sure they are using a thesis statement or embedding data using a citation, then that can be the focus of your score or feedback. As I say in *'Tween Crayons and Curfews: Tips for Middle School Teachers*, "I know there may be other mistakes, but did they absorb the one you are most focused on right now? Also, think about it from a student's point of view: if the feedback is to mean something to them, it would make a greater impact and be less defeating to see specific and targeted notes on a single topic then to see the bloody explosion of red pen all over the place (or any other color you're currently using)."

Student Exemplars

IQ Quiz

What is your name?*

[ ]

Your capacity for intelligence...
○ Does not change once you are born
○ Stops growing when you aren't in school
○ Changes over time
○ Is set permanently once you reach a certain age

List some ways to determine whether an advertisement for a mental test is reliable.

[   ]

Which of the following are methods to improve your brain's skill?
☐ Recognizing patterns and trends
☐ Building physique
☐ Practice decision-making skills
☐ Memorization
☐ Eating especially nutritious food

From a scale of 1 to 5, how effective do you think medications are to advancing your intelligence?

1 2 3 4 5
○ ○ ○ ○ ○

What does it mean when the article states that, "The brain...even the adult brain...is surprisingly plastic?"

[   ]

What areas might a mental exercise focus on?
☐ Control of attention
☐ Physical strength
☐ Creativity
☐ Ability to make connections
☐ Mathematics

Your level of intellect is a combination of both your genetics and environmental circumstances. Do you think any one factor has a stronger influence, and why?

[   ]

On a scale of 1 to 10, how important do you think education is to nurturing your intelligence?

1 2 3 4 5 6 7 8 9 10
○ ○ ○ ○ ○ ○ ○ ○ ○ ○

Compare a physical workout to a mental workout. How are they alike or different?

[   ]

What are some signs that your intelligence has improved?
☐ Able to memorize things more easily
☐ More aware of details around you
☐ Analyzing information gets harder
☐ You want to read and learn more

☐ Send me a copy of my responses.

(Submit)
Never submit passwords through Google Forms.

Jigsaw #1 Example

Warren P.

Summary: Traits like determination, tolerance, and independence are commonly found in the world's geniuses. However, on *Psychology Today*, more specifically *The Downside of Genius* written by *Roberta B. Ness* they described geniuses' personalities as a *"two sided coin."* Geniuses have a possibility to become *"arrogant or narcissistic and to engage in behaviors that are oppositional or even antisocial."* If geniuses have too much of a trait they can become something else, for example, having too much persistence may cause a genius to become a psychopath. Geniuses also began to push the limits of right and wrong. A vile example of pushing the limits is Stanley Milgram, who tricked his volunteers into thinking they were going to be put in a word-learning study. However, the subjects soon found out that they were not going to learn words, but were secretly being tested for reverence against authority. The victims were made to believe that another patient was being shocked. Sadly, the experiment didn't go as planned. 65% of the test subjects, did not try to rebel and help the patient (which was a audio recording.) Geniuses are the builders of the future, but if they go over, they may be viewed as psychopathic humans.

Questions:

1. What other overbearing traits are there in a genius?
2. Have there been other geniuses that did something as horrible as Stanley Milgram and Thomas Edison, to find truth?
3. Has anyone gotten arrested for pushing their experiments past the limit of right and wrong?
4. What examples are there for narcissistic or arrogant geniuses?
5. How did Stanley Milgram trick his volunteers so easily?

Bibliography

Ness, Roberta B. "The Downside of Genius." n.d.: n. pag. *Psychology Today*. Sussex Publishers, 13 July 2013. Web. 8 Jan. 2014.

Audry K.

Geniuses think very differently than a normal person. In The Creativity Posts' post, "How Geniuses Think" by Michael Michalko, I learned that while a normal person might face a problem and look for the most direct and simple way to solve the problem. A genius, however would put the simple solution, but they would also find answers and solutions that are unique and original. Michalko stated that, "When confronted with a problem, they ask, 'How many different ways can I look at it?', 'How can I rethink the way I see it?', and 'How many different ways can I solve this?' instead of 'What have I been taught by someone else on how to solve this?' " This kind of thinking makes genius find solutions that normal people would never have come up with or thought of. An example of genius thinking, is when Einstein was asked how he was different from normal people he answered, "If you asked the average person to find a needle in the haystack, the person would stop when he or she found a needle. I, on the other hand, would tear through the entire haystack looking for all the possible needles." Another topic that was covered was intelligence. Michalko stated that intelligence and how smart you are has nothing to do with being a genius. He believed that geniuses are people who change the world. You could be the smartest person in the room, but the one that Michalko would consider a genius is the one who is creative, thinks outside of the box, and wants to change the world. All in all, genius think differently than the average person, but it has nothing to do with how smart they are, just the fact that they want to make a difference.

Questions:

1. In the case of Marilyn von Savant, a woman who has an IQ of 228, what made her smarter than other people?
2. Do you think that being genius is about intelligence or creativity?
3. What would you do if you could make a difference in the world and be considered as genius?

Bibliography

Michalko, Michael. "How Geniuses Think." *The Creativity Post.* PaperTiger, 28 April. 2012. Web. 07 Jan. 2014.

IQ Quiz

Genius Psychological Report (Duration: 10 weeks)

January 16, 2014

Patient: Chloe T.
Age: 4 years old
Diagnosis: Genius
Patient #087
Father: Park Tran
Mother: Eleanor Tran
Reporting Doctor: Dr. Stephanie F.

To the Parent/Guardian of Chloe Tran:

Abstract—A lab report regarding patient #087, Chloe Tran. After observations and test results, I have come to a conclusion that Chloe is a gifted child. When given back her I.Q. results, after consulting the child's parents, her score came to 160, equivalent to Einstein and Stephen Hawking. She has shown outstanding intelligence in the areas of science and literature.

Introduction

After a few months meeting with your child and conducting many tests, it has come to my attention that your child, Chloe Tran has developed some unusual symptoms. First of all, when I first met with your child, she was about four years of age and had already shown signs of curiosity and creativity. Chloe would always ask very high-level questions and exhibit the desire to learn more. These characteristics were very impressive for a toddler, so I decided to experiment more with her advanced brain. Now, according to the article <u>How to Tell if your Preschooler is Gifted</u> by Jill Levey, some signs of an exceptional preschooler are

- a specific talent that demonstrates an advanced understanding of that skill;
- advanced language development;
- relentlessly asking question and analytical;
- unusually active;
- vivid imagination;
- can easily recall facts and information.

Jill Levey says, "Some gifted children realize that they are 'different' from their peers. This can make them feel isolated or withdrawn." I can definitely see that in Chloe's situation. Everytime she visits my office, she is very withdrawn from the world. She shows signs of isolated and becoming introverted.

Chloe exhibits almost all of these traits, and I can firmly conclude based on my observations from these past ten months and on my colleagues' research studies that your child inhibits all the required standards to be deemed a genius.

A genius is formally defined as an exceptionally intelligent person or one with exceptional skill in a particular area of activity. Many inventors and artists have been deemed a genius with their intelligent and unique minds. And I believe your daughter is capable of making it on this list. She has an intelligent mind with a rare knack. And with all the modern technology and research, many scientists have cracked the code between a genius's brain and the common brain.

A colleague of mine by the pseudonym, <u>GeniusisAwakening</u> dug deep into the brains of a genius and concluded that the connections in our brains and the thalamus are different. In a normal brain, there are a long and short connection in the <u>cerebral cortex</u>. Short connections usually correlate to the aptitude of something you are interested in while the long connections refers to the capacity of things outside of interests. However, in Chloe's case, her short connection seems to be longer than her long connection just like many geniuses. For example, Beethoven was born with a rare knack for music and had quite a lot of short cerebral connections. Similarly, the thalamus, or the filter in our brains, has dopamine receptors that "filter" the thoughts that are valuable and the thoughts that are stifled. But in a genius' brain, there are less dopamine receptors "thus, the neck of the bottle tends to be wider, letting more thoughts come through." This opens up more possibilities for creativity and problem solving.

Materials

The following materials were used to gather data:

- computer
- games
- observations
- Mensa test
- brain scan
- expert opinions.

Expert Opinion of issue: I had used the resources of other close friends who specialized in this area of expertise. One of which was my good friend Linda Serck, who wrote the article "Tell-Tale Signs of a Genius Child". In her article, she had included a bulleted list of the signs of a genius child. Said list included, "An unusual memory, reading early, unusual hobbies or interests or an in-depth knowledge of certain subjects, an awareness of world events, asks questions all the time, has a developed sense of humor, is musical, likes to be in control, and makes up additional rules for games." My theory was tested for a couple of weeks, five at the most. She had a high level of curiosity, always asking questions. Chloe also started reading very much, whatever she could get her hands on.

Her behaviors were more mature than what it should be for a child at her age. She started to ask an endless amount of questions, always determined to find out the answers to things and how they worked.

Results of brain scan: There also seems to be gray matter within her brain when I did a general scan of her brain. And from studies by my colleague, gray matter is present in highly-advanced brains with an adept approach of things.

Results of Mensa Test: So with all the general information I gathered for 4 weeks, I began a new experiment to really test her capability and confirm my hypothesis. I sat her in front of a computer screen and told her to take the Mensa test.

The Mensa test is a renowned program used to test individuals' IQ and brain level. Their objective is to hone all the bright intelligent minds into one society where all cards are off the table and everyone is free to be themselves. They accepted anyone whose IQ is the top 2% in their population. Their members range from 2 to more than 100. To qualify, people or students must

- take the Mensa test;
- submit a qualifying test score.

After a few weeks, Mensa gave me the results of your daughter's test scores and they were quite spectacular. Let me just break it down for you:

The Mensa program only accepts the ninety-eighth percentile. So her overall score is calculated by comparing her raw score to the scores of broad individuals who took the same test.

Chloe's raw score:

MAT(Mensa Admissions Test)= 97–120

Percentile: 99

Conclusion and Advice

For a four year old, your daughter did amazing and definitely qualified for the Mensa test. After all my examinations for ten weeks, your daughter was an exciting and bright patient. I have concluded that your daughter is indeed a bright genius with a lot of potential to influence the world and herself. Both her internal and external qualities prove how intelligent and special she is. Her test scores were very comparable to that of Albert Einstein and her behavior was very unique. Overall, she has demonstrated exceptional results.

However, I would recommend a second opinion to another specialist, as one opinion is not always correct. Might I also suggest educating yourself about geniuses. Try to obtain as much knowledge about this subject as you can. The parents need not make a hasty decision about what to do next, as one such may affect Chloe negatively instead of positively. Be aware that some genius childs are known to be bullied.

Chloe's IQ is very high. There may be a lot of opportunities for her to one day find a good job, but it is important to get advice about her health, especially with such a high thinking level. But for the parents, you should take precautions. Be prepared that . . .

1. Your child may develop behaviors such as "selfishness, self-centeredness, tolerance, . . ." said by creativity scientist Howard Gardener. Monitor her behavior, and if needed, contact a doctor when it becomes serious.
2. She may "cross the line" of acceptable scientific behavior.
3. Some health problems may occur, such as possible stress. Exercise caution if needed.

Literature Cited

Benjamin, Kathy. "11 Historical Geniuses and Their Possible Mental Disorders." *Mental Floss*. Mental Floss, 11 Sept. 2012. Web. 08 Jan. 2014. http://mentalfloss.com/article/12500/11-historical-geniuses-and-their-possible-mental-disorders
"Mensa International." *What Is Mensa?* N.p., n.d. Web. 17 Jan. a2014.
Serck, Linda. Tell-tale Signs of Genius Child. BBC News. BBC South, 14 April 2012. Web. www.bbc.co.uk/news/uk-england-hampshire-17702465

Youth Intelligence Report

Dear Parent/Guardian of Kelly Jones,

We are writing to inform you that after observing your child over the six-month course, test results have shown that your child's intelligence is much above an average person's. Kreativ Youth® has performed several different tests on your child and the results clearly show that your child may be a genius, and specifically with an outstanding aptitude in reading. Shown below, are your child's test results.

Test Results:

IQ Test
July 6, 2013
Score: 155

In the first test, which measured IQ, your child was given 30 minutes to take an online IQ test which measures logical reasoning, math skills, language abilities, ability to understand ideas, and problem-solving skills. She has demonstrated excellence in all areas that were tested, resulting in an IQ score that only 2% of the world currently scores, as shown by the charts on an IQ comparison site.

Memory Test
August 13, 2013
Score: 5 cards out of 5 cards

In the second test we performed, your child was tested of his or her memory, as having an extraordinary memory is one of the common signs that highly intelligent kids possess.

The memory test consists of 5 levels and it begins with your child being shown an easy row of five shapes. Your child was given ten seconds to look at the card and then repeat the shapes that he or she saw. In the next level, your child was read a short story and then asked what the character's name were, the animals that appeared in the story, and the places the characters went to. Finally, the last three levels of the memory test tested your child's memory with rows of objects, words, and numbers. Your child aced all five levels and clearly demonstrates a remarkable memory.

Interview
September 3, 2013

In our third test, the objective was to get to know your child better and understand your child's favorable activities and behavior to identify more signs of a genius child.

After a thirty-minute talk, we have observed characteristics that your child shares with other highly intelligent children and how each was observed:

◆ Enjoys the company of teachers.
◆ Tested by asking who your child enjoys playing with at school. She answers that it is difficult to make friends at school because they don't "understand" her. Rather, she enjoys talking with the teacher who does "understand" her. BBC News reveals that, "When genius children are invited to classmates' parties, you can guarantee they'd be in the kitchen with a cup of tea chatting with the adults—and not racing round with the other kids."
◆ Reads at a higher level.
◆ Tested by a simple question in the interview: "What do you like to do when you're at home?" and reading was one of the activities which she listed where she then continued a long conversation about his or her favorite books. Most of the books that she listed were much above an average reading level for a 12-year-old.
◆ Asks many questions.
◆ Talks a lot.
◆ Throughout the interview, your child overall had many thoughts to share.
◆ Demonstrates curiosity.
◆ Throughout the interview, topics that were new to your child were brought up, and your child showed an interest in learning new things and asked many questions.

The observations as listed above are all characteristics of a genius child, which your child demonstrates.

Learning that your child has high intelligence may be great news. However, creativity scientist, Howard Gardner from Psychology Today says, "Genius children may have their advantages, but they also have their disadvantages." As parents of a genius child, it comes with much more responsibility. Senfited.org, a gifted children's organization has proven that as highly intelligent kids grow older, they tend to:

◆ suffer depression;
◆ lie often;
◆ take drugs and alcohol.

To prevent your child of following these behaviors, we recommend that you watch your child closely by asking her about her day, observing her behavior, and keeping a close relationship with her. By doing this, you will understand what goes on in her life, reducing the chances of depression, drug-intake, and lying.

As parents of a genius child, upon hearing this news, you could also have your daughter apply for Mensa. Mensa is the largest and oldest high IQ society in the world. You can apply your child by taking the Mensa test or submitting another Intelligence test. If you are interested, you could visit www.mensa.org/.

Congratulations on your child's test result scores!

Best wishes,
Kreativ Youth®

Sources

Serck, Linda. "Tell-tale Signs of a Genius Child." *BBC News*. BBC, 14 Apr. 2012. Web. 17 Jan. 2014.
"IQ Percentile and Rarity Chart." *IQ Percentile and Rarity Chart*. N.p., n.d. Web. 17 Jan. 2014.
"Mensa International." *What Is Mensa?* N.p., n.d. Web. 17 Jan. 2014.
"Exactly What Does an IQ Test Measure?—Curiosity." *Curiosity*. N.p., n.d. Web. 17 Jan. 2014.

The Invention Unit

A Unit Based on Inventing Solutions to Common, Everyday Problems Using Persuasive Pitch Writing, Crowdsourcing, 3D Printing, and Digital Commercial Production

Table 2.1 Invention Unit Facts

Subjects Integrated	Science—engineering, design, problem solving, analysis
	Additional science is based on student choice
	Math—geometry, angles, budgeting
	Writing—persuasive pitch letter, grant writing
	Technology—various 3D design programs and drawing programs, iMovie/Animoto/Movie Maker, internet literacy for research, graphing programs, 3D printing, Tinkercad, crowdsourcing via social media
	Art—commercial production
Skills Used	Collaboration
	Problem solving
	Creativity
	Communication
	Critical thinking
	Inquiry
	Netiquette
Duration	1 month
Driving Question(s)	How can we communicate the need for an invention and use crowdsourcing to gain input from our potential buyers?
Additional Advice Included	How to quickly assess writing without taking time away from your content

Overview

Creating curriculum, and, in particular, Project Based Learning units, is like telling a story through lesson design. The story this unit tells centers on blossoming young inventors looking to solve the minor, but irritating, problems of our day-to-day life.

There are many components to the unit: brainstorming, research, development, design, cost analysis, collaboration, and pitching. Students are using art, writing, math, science, and probably countless other elements that focus on real world content and communication.

This unit asks students to think about the needs of their home and classroom environment and invent a specific item that can become a solution to a problem. It begins with the analysis of a website as a resource and model. From there, students use writing to prove the need of the items and crowdsourcing from their peers on advice that ranges on everything from the name of the product, to the retail price of the item, to the slogan. The students will use online programs to design the product and will design a website to pitch their product.

By the end of the unit, the students will write a persuasive pitch letter to a company to fund the development of the item and develop a digital commercial that would presumably be used to sell the product to the masses. If a school also has a 3D printer, one could also conclude the unit with a gallery walk of artifacts created from the students' designs.

In the spirit of PBL, this unit uses the following elements:

- role-playing
- authentic audience
- blended writing genres
- technology use
- collaboration
- critical thinking
- problem solving
- subject matter integration.

Step-by-Step Lessons

Here is a possible checklist to help pace yourself and your students through this unit. Remember to leave flexibility by adding some empty boxes that can either be used by your own assignments or even filled in with individual goals by each student.

Pacing Checklist

Date Assigned	Assignment	Deadline
	Website analysis	
	Environment needs analysis	
	Rube Goldberg homework assignment	
	Problem statement	
	Elevator speech (Twitter activity)	
	Padlet naming activity	
	Collaboration contract	
	Coming to a consensus	
	3D design	
	Cost analysis (break-even analysis)	
	Crowdsourcing—how to design a poll/survey	
	Designing a website	
	Copyrighting a website	
	Wacky product reviews Commenting on a blog	
	Writing with numeracy	
	Business letter	
	Commercial	
	Presentations	

① **Website Analysis:** One of the resources I have the kids use to prime their pumps for innovative thinking is Quirky.com. Quirky basically has three tabs in its menu bar that say it all: Invent, Influence, and Shop. You can submit an invention, shop for inventions, and—the coolest part of all—give input to influence the decisions an inventor makes as they move along their timeline toward final production. Finding Quirky was like finding a mecca of meaningfulness. It's a real world example of collaboration between people looking to solve a problem.

The following is an activity I designed as a scavenger hunt of sorts to help the students explore all the ways in which Quirky interacts with its audience. As a result of the hunt, the students also have developed the framework for their analysis of the website. In the activity, I ask students to produce a short QRF (question/response formatted answer), a question-response paragraph that incorporates evidence and commentary. The structure of a QRF is included in Part II of this book.

Website Analysis

Today, I'm going to introduce you to a new website that has an interesting premise. However, I'm not going to tell you what it is. Instead, I'm going to let you explore the site. Then tell me what you can based on your analysis of its elements. As you explore the website, think about its purpose.

Go to www.quirky.com.

Explore and Analyze
(break it down into its components)

1. Go to the "How it Works" tab at the top of the homepage. What are the 5 Steps of the Quirky process?
   1.
   2.
   3.
   4.
   5.
2. Watch the video under the "Help Us Decide" tab. Who gives feedback and input into deciding what products are produced?
3. What is the difference between the "Invent" tab and the "Influence" tab? In other words, what are each of the tabs asking you to do?
4. What is "Crowdsourcing"? Hint: if you can't figure it out, you can always Google the term. How does the term apply to Quirky?
5. Quirky is a real world application of the 4Cs: Creativity, Collaboration, Communication, and Critical Thinking. Using QRF format, pick one of those categories and dive a little deeper into describing how Quirky hits that goal.
6. What are the 3 elements of the "Invention Checklist"?
   ◆
   ◆
   ◆
7. An audience gets to help the inventor decide a number of the elements that help sell a product. What are the elements for which an audience gets to give input? Please list.

Start to Synthesize
(put the components together)

8. Go to "Shop" and explore at least 5 categories of inventions. Within those categories, what are 3 products that look particularly interesting to you?
   ◆
   ◆
   ◆

9. Think about why you are interested in those products, and then select the **ONE** you find the most interesting and write an analysis that dives more deeply into its purpose and description. Think about the following: What is so interesting about the item you chose? What do you like about the product, and what parts of the marketing pitch pulled you into looking more closely at the product? What problem does it solve? Write a QRF that answers the question: **Why do you think this particular product will be the next best thing?**

You can see a completed version of this activity in the Student Exemplars section at the end of this chapter.

2 **Environmental Needs Analysis:** From there, students need to take a good look around their homes and classrooms to think about problems that might need to be solved. I broke down into more detail where they should be looking.

Create a Needs Analysis

As a result of your hunting around and looking at other people's ideas, has this sparked any ideas of your own? Think about your own home. Go from room to room and develop a list of 3–5 problems that need to be solved in each of the major spaces of your house or apartment.

Front door/Hallway/Porch
◆
◆
◆
Living room/Den
◆
◆
◆
Bedroom(s)
◆
◆
◆
Kitchen
◆
◆
◆
Bathroom
◆
◆
◆

Outdoor area
- ◆
- ◆
- ◆

Classrooms
- ◆
- ◆
- ◆

Pet area
- ◆
- ◆
- ◆

To see an example of this activity filled out, go to the Student Exemplars at the end of this chapter.

Homework Hint

Have students look at the designs of Rube Goldberg. Have them go to www.rube-goldberg.com/ or check out YouTube videos people have made in honor of Goldberg's work. Now, while we aren't necessarily asking students to develop a machine for this unit, it is important that they understand sequence and procedure. Have students select a machine and break it down into its components, identifying each step either through writing or visual note taking. It might just help to further get those brains ready for some creative activity.

---

3 **Problem Statement:** From there, each student must write a problem statement. A problem statement is a one- to two-paragraph proof of initial research. That is, in order to write a problem statement, students needed to have conducted a least a modicum of research to prove they understand the problem and their solution has some scientific merit. They must also include a works cited and develop three to five questions that will guide them in their future research. A handout of how to write a problem statement is included in Part II of this book. See the end of the chapter for a student sample from this unit.

Developing a problem statement helps address one of the key standards clearly defined by the Next Generation Science Standards:

3–5-ETS1–1.	Define a simple design problem reflecting a need or a want that includes specified criteria for success and constraints on materials, time, or cost.

At this point in their initial research, introduce them to Instagrok, a visual research search engine. It helps to do quick, just-out-of-the-starting-gate research and can help guide deeper research later. Figure 2.1 is a screenshot of an Instagrok search about air conditioning that was conducted when a student began inquiring about the needs of her home:

Figure 2.1 Instagrok Screenshot

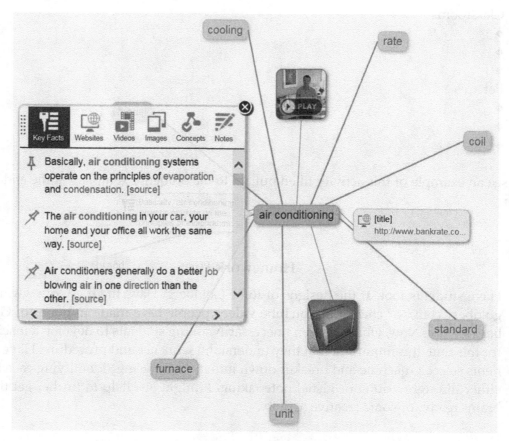

After all, the ability to conduct research is found in the standards as:

W.5.7	Conduct short research projects that use several sources to build knowledge through investigation of different aspects of a topic. (5-PS1–4)

4 **Elevator Speech (Twitter Activity):** Once students have developed their problem statements, you want to train them in how to boil them down to their gist. Have them develop an elevator speech of their product. As I said in the introduction of this book, an elevator speech is an encapsulated version of what they are trying to say that must fit in the short time it would takes to pitch the concept on an elevator riding between two floors.

Here's an example of my student Jacob's elevator speech:

Jacob B: I have invented something called The Smart Drawer. It is very efficient and will solve all the problems that today's society has with drawers. Whether you struggle with a disability or simply have your hands full, our Smart Drawer application will help. A sensor on our drawers reads a corresponding sensor on a floor pad that will make it open instantly when you stand on it. The Smart Drawer can even tell you when you have too many items or clothes in it to shut properly. Here's my card should you wish to reach me!

You might even want to challenge students to pare it down even more. Using the Twitter-like strategy of allowing them only 140 characters or fewer, have students use Todaysmeet to present their elevator speeches. After all, pitching a product using Twitter is not inconceivable in today's world.

Todaysmeet.com works exactly like Twitter except you can "close the room" or shut down the feed after a certain amount of time.

Here's Jacob's speech boiled down even further:

Here is the Smart Drawer. If your hands are full or you can't open the drawer, a sensor on the floor will help you solve your problems! = 135 characters

The ability to summarize is a requirement defined under the literacy standards in the science and technical subjects that can be found in the Common Core Standards:

CCSS.ELA-LITERACY.RST.6–8.2
Determine the central ideas or conclusions of a text; provide an accurate summary of the text distinct from prior knowledge or opinions.

Incorporate summarizing into this science-based unit and you will be supporting both literacy and writing.

5 **Collaboration Contract:** Now, depending on your goal for this unit, each individual student can design their own product, or students can work in groups and select a product from the problem statements written independently. A collaborative contract is a document that is constructed by all stakeholders in a small group. It lists the expectations they might have in working together, the process they agreed upon in reaching out to each other, perhaps the frequency in which they agree to meet, and so forth. If the students have not set these expectations ahead of time, they cannot hold each other accountable for their work in the same way. My collaboration contract assignment (sometimes called the collaboration constitution) can be found in Part II of this book.

6 **Coming to a Consensus:** Having trouble watching the kids disagree on their collaboration constitutions or problem statements? Teach them how to come to a consensus. In my earlier book, *'Tween Crayons and Curfews: Tips for Middle School Teachers*, I talk a lot about the need to build community and guide students in more academic communication skills. Giving students strategies to help make decisions, like needing to come to a consensus, is vital if you are trying to build up those communication muscles.

In the book, I say:

Once you buy-in to small groups, you have to teach them the language of getting along. As we know, problem solving requires making decisions, and making decisions in a community (even a small group of 5) and reaching consensus with a group is hard even for adults. Now imagine you're a student in a group that consists of someone you have a crush on, someone you hate, someone who's shy, and someone who's overbearing. Your teacher gives you a task and a timed deadline and says, "Solve!"

It wouldn't be fair, and it wouldn't be effective. Therefore, we have to scaffold how to be fair in a group or small groups won't work. I really feel for teachers who excuse their lack of utilizing this powerful strategy, claiming that small group work isn't fair to the high achievers or that it somehow allows underachievers to continue to float under the radar. These aren't reasons enough not to tackle that which makes a richer environment. Rather, they are reasons to solve those problems instead.

To reach a consensus requires work from every member of the group and a way to hold each member accountable.

Here is one strategy I use to encourage more equitable work and discussion:

1. Have the students each write a paragraph stating their opinion and their most important reason.
2. Pass around these papers among the members of the group so everyone reads everyone's contributions and everyone has input.
3. Have someone tally the student's opinions to find out what the majority believes.
4. Allow someone from the minority opinion to make a final argument.
5. Vote one at a time: ballots, show of hands, etc.
6. Move on as soon as the decision has been made.

7 **Padlet Naming Activity:** Padlet is a quick and easy program to use in order to get a quick temperature of the room. In this case, I use it to make sure that certain decisions are made by certain times in order to keep the decision-making process moving along. For instance, I ask the students to decide on the working names for their products within a very quick time period. Sure, these names can change as the student continues his or her research and development, but it's really important that students don't get hung up on certain decisions for too long or it gums up the works, so to speak.

Figure 2.2 is a screenshot of a Padlet wall after my students had brainstormed names for their products. It took no more than one minute to set up. I sent the link to the students, and they entered the names sometime throughout the class period. By the end of class, this served as an exit card of sorts, telling me they had at least figured out this element of the overall assignment.

8 **3D Design:** There are some great programs out there that can help students bring their inventions to fruition. The Quirky.com folks suggest sketching out products first and making cardboard prototypes next. Then students can get into more 3D possibilities. Programs like Tinkercad and 123Design can create 3D representations while programs like Paper or Sketchbook can help students create simple drawings of their products. From there, once students design their eventual promotional website, they can include a link to the interactive design they created or can embed a screenshot of the image.

Figure 2.2 Padlet Screenshot

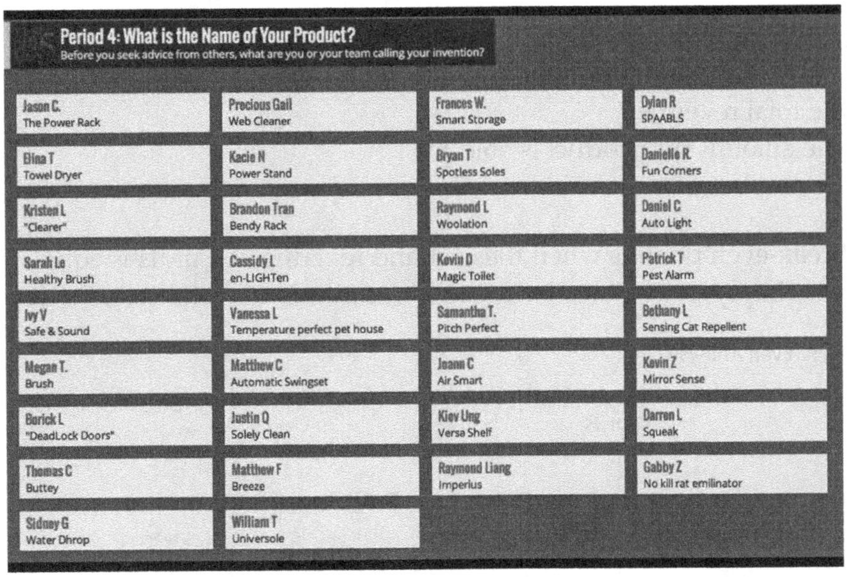

Creating a mock prototype prior to final design is a key component of this problem-solution unit. This addresses the Next Generation Science Standards here:

3–5-ETS1–1.	Define a simple design problem reflecting a need or a want that includes specified criteria for success and constraints on materials, time, or cost.

Simultaneously, it also hits the Common Core mathematical standards as it requires of all grade levels "model with mathematics . . . using appropriate tools" through using visual and concrete models to produce a solution.

9 **Cost Analysis (Break-Even Analysis):** Eric Hoenigmann, the department chair at my local high school and a great teacher who loves Project Based Learning, developed a lesson that helps students figure out the real world cost to produce a product versus the retail value of that product. This kind of activity is valuable for many kinds of PBL units. Hoenigmann calls it the break-even analysis. Regarding this lesson, Hoenigmann says the following: "A break-even analysis allows you to determine how many product units you must sell before you begin to make a profit."

The formula for the cost of producing your product per unit is:

$$C = mx + b$$

C is the total cost
m is the cost to produce each unit
x is the number of units produced
b is the initial manufacturing cost

The formula for the revenue generated is:

$R = mx$

R is the total revenue
m is the amount the product is sold for
x is the number of units sold

The break-even point is when the cost and revenue of x units is equal, C = R.
Profit is simply determined by the revenue minus the total cost, P = R − C.

Figure 2.3 The Break-Even Analysis

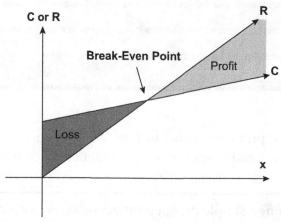

Hoenigmann then goes on to ask his students to use writing to answer the following questions:

What are the cost and revenue models for your product?
How many units must you sell to make a profit? In other words, what is the break-even point?

He says that students can create a graph like the one in Figure 2.3 for their own product break-even analysis at www.desmos.com.
An example is provided in Figure 2.4.
Using desmos.com, and using it to define an equation that analyzes the cost to produce versus the cost to sell, is covered in many Common Core math standards. For instance:

CCSS.MATH.CONTENT.7.EE.B.4
Use variables to represent quantities in a real-world or mathematical problem, and construct simple equations and inequalities to solve problems by reasoning about the quantities.

Additionally, when we talk about modeling at the high school level, the standards state the following:

It involves (1) identifying variables in the situation and selecting those that represent essential features, (2) formulating a model by creating and selecting geometric,

Figure 2.4 Graph for Break-Even Analysis

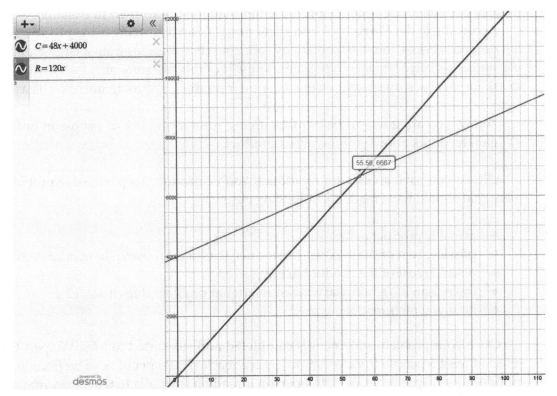

graphical, tabular, algebraic, or statistical representations that describe relationships between the variables, (3) analyzing and performing operations on these relationships to draw conclusions, (4) interpreting the results of the mathematics in terms of the original situation, (5) validating the conclusions by comparing them with the situation, and then either improving the model or, if it is acceptable, (6) reporting on the conclusions and the reasoning behind them.

Specifically, using "appropriate tools" such as desmos.com to accomplish these goals addresses the following:

Graphing utilities, spreadsheets, computer algebra systems, and dynamic geometry software are powerful tools that can be used to model purely mathematical phenomena (e.g., the behavior of polynomials) as well as physical phenomena.

10 **Crowdsourcing—How to Design a Poll/Survey:** The next step of the design process is to get feedback from peers on certain decisions before they are finalized. To do that, however, students need to know how to design engaging surveys and polls in order to collect their feedback or data. More information on the kinds of questions you can have students develop can be found in the "Teach the Teacher Unit."

Students love to give their opinions. Therefore, it's vital to leverage their nature in every subject area, and it's really important to allow this step in the design process. Besides, not only do we collaborate in classrooms for students to grow in their ability to communicate, we also use it because what results is greater than having worked in isolation.

According to the *Merriam Webster* dictionary, "**Crowdsourcing** is the process of obtaining needed services, ideas, or content by soliciting contributions from a large group of people, and especially from an online community." For this assignment, the students will have to ask for feedback on specific elements of their product. The assignment reads as follows:

> Today, you are going to be crowdsourcing from a number of people in order to gain feedback about your invented product.

> OK, so you have an idea for a product. You've produced a persuasive problem statement that should have made the following clear:

> - possible product name;
> - possible cost of the product to produce (based on research of similar items);
> - possible cost of the product to buy;
> - the reason it's a necessary invention (what problem does it solve?);
> - how you picture it being used.

Once your problem statement is completed and submitted to Mrs. Wolpert-Gawron, select at least 5 people from whom to get feedback. These people can be from any of the Honors classes (periods 4, 6, 7). **If a person already has 5 polls to take, they may not take more, and you need to reach out to other individuals for feedback.**

To create a poll, you will be developing a Google Form.

You are asking for feedback on the following elements. (You may ask for other feedback as well, but remember that you are taking up a person's time, so make sure your questions are necessary.)

Format of the Poll

The problem statement (with works cited) should be included at the top of the poll or sent in an individual email. Your audience needs to read it in order to respond to your poll.

You are getting feedback on the following:

1. Name
2. Retail cost (is it a reasonable amount to expect people to spend?)
3. Slogan (advice on a saying that captures the spirit and purpose of the product)
4. Opinion of the need for this product (in other words, ask them how important they believe it to be—their answer will probably be determined by how convincing/persuasive you were in your problem statement!)

The students can use the different formats of questioning they learned to get the feedback they need from their peers.

Once you have gathered the feedback from your online peers, you need to compile the information into a document that SYNTHESIZES how they responded and whether or not you took any of their advice.

This document, which is an analysis of sorts, is due, in essay form (but can also include the screenshot of a table or any other graphic you think will highlight your points), on _____.

⑪ Designing a Website: By the end of the unit, students will have created a website to house their assignments and artifacts they've been designing all through this unit. This serves to promote their product and integrate some valuable persuasive writing techniques.

Website design also hits some key 21st-century skills and strategies that are necessary for our students to learn. Such organizations as the Institute of Museum and Library Services call for students to do the following:

Manage Projects (Productivity and Accountability)
◆ Set and meet goals, even in the face of obstacles and competing pressures.
◆ Prioritize, plan and manage work to achieve the intended result.

Manage Goals and Time (Initiative and Self-Direction)
◆ Set goals with tangible and intangible success criteria.
◆ Balance tactical (short-term) and strategic (long-term) goals.
◆ Utilize time and manage workload efficiently.

In fact, the guys at Quirky.com also believe that presentation and promotion are important steps in the invention process. They say, "Inventors can create their own blogs to promote their inventions, work with assistance programs such as Dragon Innovation in Boston, or share them with online communities such as Thingiverse, Instructables, and Behance."

My students, however, created websites using Weebly, Wix, eMaze, and Google Sites. Their pages informed and argued using text, data, description, and original 3D designs. We even wrote reviews of our products mimicking those we saw for household items on Amazon.

We looked at websites like the one for As Seen On TV for inspiration and for fun.

Here was the actual assignment I shared with my students:

While I intend for you to start working on this on Monday in class, the fact is that some of you might want to start tinkering with your website design as early as this weekend. No pressure, but I thought I'd send this early to allow for those who want to get started.

Next, you are going to begin working on a website to promote your invented product. Have fun with this! The website itself should be completed by Friday, January 30. After all, you have much of the writing already completed. On Friday, peers will be commenting and leaving a review of your product, so make sure you're ready to receive visitors!

1. Homepage
   Final image of the product (check out Tinkercad or Autodesk 123D if you want; see the following for more advice on creating the visual for your product)

Name of the product

Slogan

Any persuasive ad elements (Buy now!, As Seen on TV!, etc.)

2. Collaboration Contract

If you worked in a group, the contract must be posted on its own page along with a page for each individual member. Color code by students for this assignment to indicate which student contributed what, so that it is obvious who is doing the work and who is not.

3. Basic Facts

Purpose, Anecdotal?

Price

4. Manufacturing Process

Step-by-step process of inventing the product, including quotes from your crowdsourcing, brainstorming process, revision description, cost analysis (how did you come to its price point?), blueprint, etc., and spreadsheet (if you did the extra credit)

Link to problem statement (should include works cited)

Business letter (final draft should have hyperlinks, works cited, etc. and should be visible on website)

You can repurpose past assignments and tweak prior activities or link to other files to communicate the steps through this unit; this page should also include links or embedded documents such as the problem statement and the business letter

5. Reviews

Image of product

Allow peers to comment on this page

Suggestion: graphics a la Amazon to reflect ratings, stars, customers who viewed this item also bought, etc.

6. Research Library

Members combined and listed all their bibliographical research in proper MLA or APA format

7. Infomercial (only if you did the extra credit)

See the student samples at the end of this chapter for some screenshots of websites created by my students.

12 **Copyrighting a Website:** Online ethics is about respecting other people's work. This lesson can be reinforced by also showing students how they can respect their own work. Talk to the students about licensing and how copyright laws are there to protect an innovative creator like themselves by disallowing another person to use their ideas without permission.

It's a fine line: we are encouraging collaboration but not the taking of ideas without consent. It might seem straightforward to us, the teachers and other adults, but for a student who has grown up with online access to the world's ideas, there might seem no distinction. So I show students how to recognize different copyright marks and how to license their own work.

Have them go to www.creativecommons.org. Show them the licensing feature and how to put a free license on their own invention websites. It's an easy click, cut, and paste process, and students really understand the options that are offered. It's amazing how tight a license the kids will want for their own sites! Figure 2.5 is a picture of the Creative Commons license my student put on his website to battle anyone who might want to modify or sell his work without permission.

13 **Wacky Product Reviews:** One of the elements of this Invention Unit is in understanding how persuasive writing relates to the invention and marketing process. One kind of persuasive writing students can be exposed to is in the writing of reviews. Have students look at the real world product reviews on Amazon. Products like the Banana Slicer or the Hawaii Chair have some humorous satire consumers have used in reviewing the product. Look at the reviews ahead of time to check current appropriateness, but, in general, looking at these reviews can prove both educational from a persuasive lens and downright entertaining.

Homework Hint

Have students check out particular reviews and assess the writing they see on persuasive techniques. Does the reviewer recommend the product or not? How vehement are their word choices? Do they include evidence or concrete examples that prove their point?

---

14 **Commenting on a Blog:** Once the websites have been created to promote the product, have the students tour them and "review" them as if they had purchased the product. Have them read the problem statements, look at the images, and read the persuasive language. Then have them write reviews that either try to persuade readers to purchase or avoid the product. Make sure they write using evidence based on the realities of the product itself.

Frontload the assignment by going over some norms on how to comment on a blog so that students are constructive in tone. See Part II of this book for a handout on those norms.

Figure 2.5 Creative Commons License

Brandon T.

This product is the best! Since I'm so lazy and refuse to turn off my lights because they're too far away, this product helps a lot! Not only do you get to be lazy, you get to save money while being lazy. It's the best possible thing that I could ever hope for. Despite its complex appearance, the Light Genius is very simple to use. All you have to do is stick it on your wall next to your light, walk past the motion sensor, and the Light Genius does everything else for you! Buy one now, before they run out of stock! 5/5

Bethany L.

I love this product! Ever since I purchased it, going to the restroom has been a lot more fun. I can listen to my favorite radio stations while in the bathroom, and I love how the QuickFlush flushes and plunges itself. Very convenient. This product is totally worth the extra money!

Vincent L.

Nowadays, people let their pets poop on other people's lawns and most of the times, they don't even pick it up or throw it away! It just stays there on the lawn, and although it might be good for the soil, it's definitely not good for the people. I myself live in a neighborhood with tons of dogs, especially those pesky Chihuahuas, and it is just frustrating to wake up one morning, go outside for a walk . . . and then see clumps of dark sausages on the lawn. Just the thought of picking it up is enough to make me go back to bed, and the worst part is, if I don't pick it up, no one else will either. However, I have recently checked out The Poop Repeler online and after I heard about how it repels animals from marking their territory on lawns, I immediately bought it. Part of the reason I did so was its amazingly cheap price for something so useful to me and other people on the street! When I first used it, I easily sprayed and covered the whole yard with the spray, and at first, it just looked like the grass was wet. However, after an entire week, I woke up to a clean, untouched lawn that never lost its natural fragrance. This product is definitely worth it, and is very unique!

15 **Writing with Numeracy:** We talk a lot about students needing to embed evidence into their writing, but are we specifically teaching how to write using numbers? To counter what I felt was a gap in my own practice, I researched how mathematicians and scientists and those in higher education were solving this problem. I found a handful of rules many of them follow (and a few that were specific to particular content areas). I combined them into a reference sheet for students and tacked on a few questions for them to answer that forced them to interact and refer to the cheat sheet I'd created. You can see it in Part II of this book.

Students need to embed data and numbers into their writing. It's a form of evidence-based communication. And while the Common Core Standards clearly require more evidence-based writing, common sense does too.

16 **Business Letter:** The culminating writing piece that students will develop is a business letter to potential investors. Have students research CEOs or company owners who represent similar devices or products. Have them write formal business letters to get them more agile with this really important college- and career-applicable writing genre. An outline for a business letter can be found in Part II of this book.

See the end of this chapter for a student sample of this assignment.

Another culminating written option that students can create is the executive summary. The executive summary is an informational pitch to an executive told in a simple way. For more details on the executive summary, go to Part II of this book for an outline.

17 **Commercial:** You can have students also use programs like iMovie to product short commercials or infomercials. Have students look at the persuasive nature of these ads and showcase their commercials to other classrooms. Have the peers be their own authentic audience.

18 **Presentation:** When tackling an invention unit, there are great opportunities to showcase student work to an audience greater than yourself. To begin with, your school can host an Invention Convention. Think of it like an invention-focused science fair. Invite local STEM professionals to help evaluate the products. Perhaps the inventions that score the highest evaluations can even be submitted to Quirky for possible consideration or to the Scholastic Klutz contest as representatives from the school.

✎ Tip on How to Assess Writing Quickly #2

Let them do the work by using an oral feedback sheet. One day I woke up and realized that students don't read any of our traditionally written feedback anymore. Upon realizing that, I became obsessed with making my advice sticky, "gluing" it somehow to my students' consciousness in a way that my handwriting did not. Eventually I asked myself . . . why am I the one taking the notes? Is not the one who does the work doing the learning?

So I developed the oral feedback sheet. It's a template for note taking that the student uses while in conference with the teacher while the class is working independently on parts of their project.

Set a timer, sit down with each kid, and hand over the job of note taking while you give oral feedback. It's valuable, and the oral feedback sheet has proven to be more effective than traditional feedback.

See Part II of this book for my oral feedback sheet.

Student Exemplars

Carlos P.—Website and Needs Analysis

Explore and Analyze
(break it down into its components)

1. **Go to the "How it Works" tab at the top of the homepage. What are the 5 Steps of the Quirky process?**
   1. Submit your idea.
   2. Help us decide.

3. Influence & learn.
4. We make it real.
5. The world prospers.

2. **Watch the video under the "Help Us Decide" tab. Who gives feedback and input into deciding what products are produced?**
Experts in industry, friends of Quirky officials, and Quirky community members give feedback and input on the products proposed.

3. **What is the difference between the "Invent" tab and the "Influence" tab? In other words, what are each of the tabs asking you to do?**
The difference between the Invent and Influence tabs is that they ask for your ideas on different things. The Invent tab asks for your own original ideas; in other words it asks you to submit your own ideas for inventions. This differs from the Influence tab, which instead asks you to help add to or give feedback on other people's designs. Basically, Invent asks you to make an invention, while Influence asks you to help make an invention better.

4. **What is "Crowdsourcing"? Hint: if you can't figure it out, you can always Google the term. How does the term apply to Quirky.com?**
Crowdsourcing is when people ask for advice on a project from a varied group of people. This directly relates to Quirky.com, as crowdsourcing is one of the most important parts of their process. They get input from experts and friends on the ideas people submit, allowing them to choose the most promising ones to focus on. They also ask their users to help influence these designs, and help improve them. Overall Quirky.com uses crowdsourcing to help refine every idea submitted to them.

5. **Quirky is a real world application of the 4Cs: Creativity, Collaboration, Communication, and Critical Thinking. Using QRF format, pick one of those categories and dive a little deeper into describing how Quirky hits that goal.**
Quirky heavily stresses the use of collaboration in its design. This is shown through the "Help Us Decide" and "Influence and Earn" steps of the Quirky process. Both of these steps require not just the person who pitched an invention to work, but other users of the site as well. Take note of the word "influence" in the evidence. By definition, influence means to give feedback and advice on something to change it or make it better. This means that it requires more than one person, and when more than a single individual work on something they're collaborating. In addition to helping improve inventions, Quirky also asks you to help them decide what innovation should get focus. This is perhaps the biggest clue to how important collaboration is on Quirky. Asking the users to decide what they should fund and spend their time on is a big show of trust, and reliance on others; it shows cooperation. In conclusion, collaboration is the overall foundation of the Quirky process.

6. **What are the 3 elements of the "Invention Checklist"?**
   ◆ Pitch your ideas.
   ◆ Give a description.
   ◆ Add visual.

7. **An audience gets to help the inventor decide a number of the elements that help sell a product. What are the elements for which an audience gets to give input? Please list.**
   ◆ Research
   ◆ Design

- ◆ Enhancements
- ◆ Style
- ◆ Name
- ◆ Tagline
- ◆ Price

Start to Synthesize
(put the components together)

8. **Go to "Shop" and explore at least 5 categories of inventions. Within those categories, what are 3 products that look particularly interesting to you?**
   - ◆ Laptop Table
   - ◆ Hydro Hand
   - ◆ Melody Squares

9. **Think about why you are interested in those products, and then select the ONE you find the most interesting and write an analysis that dives more deeply into its purpose and description. Write a QRF that answers the question: Why do you think this particular product will be the next best thing?**

   I think that the Hydro Hands (an innovation for drinking water on the go) might be the next big thing as it solves a major issue for runners and people exercising in general. This is shown when the creator stated, "The "Hydro Hands" will be used by simply just lifting up your hand and drinking from the hydro hand". This detail shows the number one advantage the hydro hands have in comparison to simple water bottles, convenience. The fact is, when you're running with water in hand, you have to stop or at least slow down a bit to drink from it. The hydro hands eliminate this issue by giving a simple motion of raising your hand to drink, not affecting pace or motion at all. This matters because when running or exercising in general, consistency is very important. If you break your tempo or pattern, you might end up injuring yourself or messing up your movements. For example, in my own experience, if I slow down my speed when running, it becomes very hard to reach that level again. This is what makes the hydro hands so versatile. It offers hydration, without interrupting your exercise. In conclusion, the "Hydro Hands" allow athletes to stay hydrated and cool, while at the same time not hindering them.

Create

10. **As a result of your hunting around and looking at other people's ideas, has this sparked any ideas of your own? Think about your own home. Go from room to room and develop a list of 3–5 problems that need to be solved in each of the major spaces of your house or apartment.**

    Front door/Hallway/Porch
    - ◆ Broken lock
    - ◆ Short door (leaves & such get in)
    - ◆ Dirty

Living room/Den
- ◆ Fireplace doesn't have funnel
- ◆ Air conditioner too weak
- ◆ Power outlets in the way

Bedroom(s)
- ◆ Closet door broken
- ◆ More space for clothes
- ◆ Supplies like pencils and pens lying around

Kitchen
- ◆ Lights run out of power quickly
- ◆ Counter space
- ◆ Utensil space

Bathroom
- ◆ Leaky pipes
- ◆ Shampoo and soap randomly placed
- ◆ Floor mat gets really wet

Outdoor area
- ◆ Need more plants
- ◆ Cracked pavement
- ◆ Sprinklers not working

Problem Statement

Most kids these days suffer from bad eyesight. The main cause for this is because they spend late nights reading in the dark or playing on their mobile devices in the dark. This problem could easily be fixed by the auto-brightness lights. This device is connected to the wall and can control all the lights in the house. It's main purpose is to read the lighting outside, and adjust the lights inside the house to the perfect lighting. This will come in handy but another problem arises. If someone were reading, they would need extra light so their eyes don't strain. Problem solved. There will be an option on the device to make a certain light brighter or dimmer than the others. According to the article, "Is reading in the dark bad for your eyesight", reading in the dark can cause your eyes to strain to catch the words. Even though your eyes have adjusted to the darkness and you can't tell that you're straining your eyes, you are. I know what it is like to get so caught up in a book that you don't realize how hard you're actually concentrating on the words. I currently suffer from nearsightedness due to reading in dim light for almost a year now. This is also caused by playing on mobile devices in the dark. Auto-brightness lights main cause is to help kids, like me, prevent from straining their eyes by reading. In the future, we will keep creating new technology, which will also increase the amount of kids spending nights on their electronics. With the auto-brightness lights, kids will get to play without having to worry too much about getting nearsightedness. This is a problem we need to tackle because, if kids have bad eyesight, they won't be able to see and learn during class. It will soon affect their grades, and all America wants is for their people to prosper. We cannot prosper if our children are suffering from nearsightedness.

1. How would the device be attached to a wall and be able to reach all the lights in the house? Will there have to be more than one device in the house?

2. How does straining your eyes lead to nearsightedness? What is the science behind it?
3. How much would it cost to install the special lights and device?
4. Would the device reading the outside light act like a solar-panel? If so, how does it work?
5. In the future, will it be possible to cure nearsightedness?

Works Cited

"Is Reading in the Dark Bad for Your Eyesight?" *BBC Future*. 01 Oct. 2012. Web. 01 Apr. 2015. <www.bbc.com/future/story/20121001-should-you-read-in-the-dark>.

Business Letter

1372 E. Las Tunas Drive
San Gabriel, CA 91776
1/22/2015

John Fry
4000 Air Park Cove Memphis
Memphis, TN 28118

Dear Mr. John Fry

I am writing to you today to ask you to help fund the creation of my invention. The name of my invention is the Dust Mite. The Dust Mite is an automatic vacuum dedicated to cleaning dust. The reason I chose to ask you to fund my project is because Fry's Electronics is "the" superstore for electronics. Fry's Electronics is filled with unique electronics and I was hoping you could make some space for my Dust Mite.

The Dust Mite isn't just an automatic vacuum dedicated to cleaning dust, it can also fly and clear the air of dust and harmful particles before they hit the surfaces in a home or office. The Dust Mite is the future of vacuuming and dusting, and it will eventually replace vacuums and dusters.

The Dust Mite is basically a quadcopter with a high power vacuum tube coming out of the bottom of the device. The high power vacuum tube will pick up every last piece of dust and will guarantee that there will not be leakage of any sort that will allow the dust to escape. I plan on sending Dust Mites to major mining companies, so that it can suck up deadly dusts such as coal dust. This can prevent the spread of diseases such as lung cancer.

Now I know what you may be thinking about the automatic vacuum part (been there, done that), but what separates mine from the iRobot (a type of automatic vacuum) is that mine can fly. Most vacuums only pick up dirt and grime on the ground, but mine can also suck up particles in the air, particles that no one likes such as pollen, dust, viruses, smoke, etc. Vacuums don't usually pick these particles up, they usually just spread them, so that is how my Dust Mite is better than all other vacuums.

Please help fund for my project, I guarantee that it will be the future of vacuuming. The Dust Mite will make you a huge profit in your store, but it will also help make the customers happy because it works so much better than just your normal vacuum. It's a win-win situation, so what do you have to lose? This project will become a reality when you fund its creation.

Sincerely,

Kevin Y.

Student Website Sample

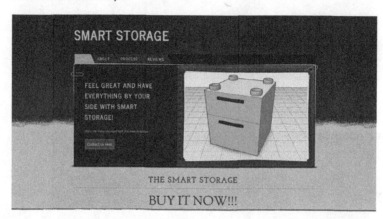

The Galapagos Unit

A Unit Committed to Funding a Mission to Save the Endangered and Unique Species of the Galapagos Islands Based on Student Research, Role-Playing, Writing an Executive Summary of Recommendations, and an Oral Pitch to the "Board" of a Major Institute

Table 3.1 Galapagos Unit Facts

Subjects Integrated	Science—growth and development of organisms, interdependent relationships in ecosystems, study of traits, natural selection, biodiversity Additional science is based on student choice Math—budgeting Writing—executive summary Reading—informational websites and journal articles Technology—Google Drive, website design, internet literacy for research, presentations, hyperlinking Art—scientific travel journal Oral presentation
Skills Used	Collaboration Problem solving Creativity Communication Critical thinking Questioning
Duration	1–2 months
Driving Question(s)	How do endangered species relate to humans, and how can we save them from extinction? How do we save the last of a species in a world that may be evolved beyond them?

Overview

This month-long unit requires the students to role-play as scientists sent to different islands of the Galapagos to research the ecosystems and their unique species. They are first challenged by the head of a national institute (this can be an iMovie of an older student, a teacher, or even a real scientist volunteering their time) to travel to a Galapagos Island of their choice to study one indigenous species of that location. They must return to the mainland with a completed scientific journal, complete with sketches and observations, that they must then convert into an oral presentation to the "board" of the institute to convince its members that their species is vital to our global needs and, thus, must be saved from extinction.

This unit was initially designed in conjunction with a brilliant seventh grade science teacher, Diane Tom, who wanted some advice about dipping her toe into Project Based Learning. She approached me at the start of a quarter looking for ways to engage all learners and make her evolution unit more real world and rigorous. What was created was a skeletal version of the unit you are about to read. We sat down and created the primary outline of the unit together, but my passion for what she was doing took over soon thereafter. The unit in this chapter reflects our collaboration and the curriculum and pacing I designed as a result of those initial brainstorms.

In the true spirit of PBL, this unit covers the following elements:

- role-play
- bringing an outside expert into the classroom
- authentic audiences
- student choice
- oral presentation
- technology
- integrating different subject areas
- The 4 Cs
- real world connections
- advocacy
- problem solving.

Step-by-Step Lessons

As I've written about earlier in this book, I generally begin with a checklist of sorts so that all stakeholders (parents, students, etc.) understand the overall method to my madness. This transparency helps preemptively answer some questions about the unit and helps students manage their time as we progress through the lessons.

Pacing Checklist

Date assigned	Assignment	Deadline
	Entry Level Event	
	Forming Exploration Groups	
	Internet literacy: Using Instagrok for visual research	
	Internet literacy: Using Google Advanced Search	
	Internet literacy: Using Google News	
	Internet literacy: Common sense	
	Inquiry: Suggest questions to help guide their research/ Cornell Notes	
	Choosing an island using Padlet	
	Collaboration contract	
	Island research	
	Biodiversity lesson	

	Punnett Square assignment	
	Bring in an expert from outside the classroom	
	The study of extinction	
	Species design	
	Digital explorers' journal	
	Oral presentation	
	Save the species selection	

1 Entry Event: The entry event to this unit could be a movie from an older student or perhaps a willing adult role-playing as the head of the board at a scientific institute. Figure 3.1 is a screenshot from my eighth grader, Benny, who quickly whipped together an iMovie that was sent to the participating seventh grade class in order to get them in the spirit of their own soon-to-be role-play.

Script for the iMovie

Greetings, Explorers. For the past 40 years, we at the Smithsonian have been tirelessly working to raise the funds necessary to send a team of researchers to explore the Galapagos Islands for the purpose of research and discovery. You have been selected to be one of those scientists to explore one of these islands and help us better understand the environment and the inhabitants of each of these islands. Your costs of travel and well being will be fully covered, I assure you, and all that we ask is that you provide us with your mind and your effort. Help us to decide which of these species we should save from extinction. It is up to you and your extensive research to convince the funding board where to spend their money and resources. Please send us your explorers' journal and your convincing analysis of your findings to help us make our decision. Good luck on your journey and God speed.

Figure 3.1 Screenshot for Benny's iMovie

Use Google Earth to fly into the Galapagos from your current location. Allow students to see just where the island chain is on our planet. This is where their team is being "sent."

The teacher should then clarify that each of the kids will be a part of an exploration team. Each team will select an island to research and study. By the end of the unit, each team will be expected to submit the following:

- a collaborative explorers' journal;
- an executive summary complete with recommendations;
- an oral presentation.

A panel of peers and adult representatives that will role-play as the Smithsonian's executive board will assess the oral presentations and written/created artifacts. These people will eventually be the ones to decide which species to help save from extinction.

2 **Forming Exploration Groups:** There are many ways to create small groups in your classroom. They all have pros and cons. Think about the goals of each unit and also about when it takes place in the school year to determine what works for you. Just some thoughts here:

Heterogeneous groups: the groups are mixed in their levels. The thing to remember when students panic (because, let's face it, they know who will pull their weight and who won't) is that the assignments are created to allow for individual grading. Nobody will be dependent on another for his or her overall grade.

Homogenous groups: the groups are made based on similarities of levels. My thought on this: meh. Sure, you can create some groups knowing there will be those who accomplish what they need and a couple that won't, but I don't think that helps any of the stakeholders. However, the plus here is that you can give more individual attention and scaffolding to kids who are grouped together knowing that other groups might be fine working more independently.

Student choice: I always tend to like a certain level of student choice in selecting groups. I do set some rules and limitations that help guide their choices, but choices lead to ownership.

Teacher choice: This is certainly more equitable and can alleviate the stress some kids feel when wondering if their peers would choose them.

Fluid grouping: As I say in my book, *'Tween Crayons and Curfews: Tips for Middle School Teachers*, I'm a fan of fluid grouping as well because it's so easy to morph into different group combinations. You can also support your content as well. I tell the students that each desk within each table group has an assigned name in accordance to our curriculum. For instance, I label each of the desks in a table with a character in literature. It's just my way of further integrating my content. Whatever your content, name your desks Pythagoras, Mycenae, Π, or Perimeter; go to town.

See Figure 3.2 for the diagram of one such table group that I use for an ELA class.

Figure 3.2 Diagram of Table Group

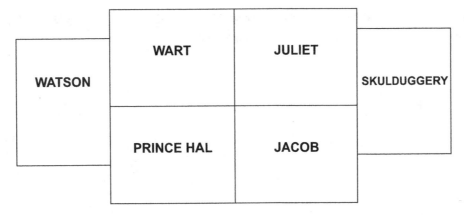

By labeling the desks at the table groups, I can create easy, fluid groups. Fluid groups are ever-changing small groups that are set up to lose no instructional time when morphing. I can say things like:

"All Juliets please go get your table's Works in Progress folders."
"All Warts get together and decide on a thesis statement."
"During this silent read, could I see all Skullduggerys over here for a brief meeting?"

It's all about integration opportunities and making the most out of every moment of instructional time. It's also about mixing up the students with fluidity and creating a tighter community. And that community will help your class run more efficiently.

3 **Internet Literacy: Using Instagrok for Visual Research:** Have the teams use the program Instagrok to do some initial research on which island to select from the Galapagos chain. For an example of what an Instagrok search looks like, go to the Invention Unit (chapter 2). In this case, give them a guided question to help their research, something like:

What are the main islands that make up the Galapagos?
Why is studying the Galapagos so important to our understanding of evolution?

4 **Choosing an Island Using Padlet:** At the end of the island research activity (which could take one to three classroom periods) have a representative from each group enter their island selection onto a Padlet wall. Project the Padlet onto the screen at the front of the room so that each group can see what islands will be involved in the unit of study and what groups will become the experts in what locations.

Padlet.com is super easy to set up and is great to use as an exit card or simply to take the temperature in a room.

Figure 3.3 is a screenshot of a classroom with a bunch of separate table groups all claiming different islands.

To avoid an overlap of islands, you can assign them or ask a short series of questions between the groups that might want to take on the same island. Whichever group researches the answers the quickest and the most completely (maybe using Google Advanced Search) can continue researching that island.

Figure 3.3 Separate Table Groups Claiming Different Islands

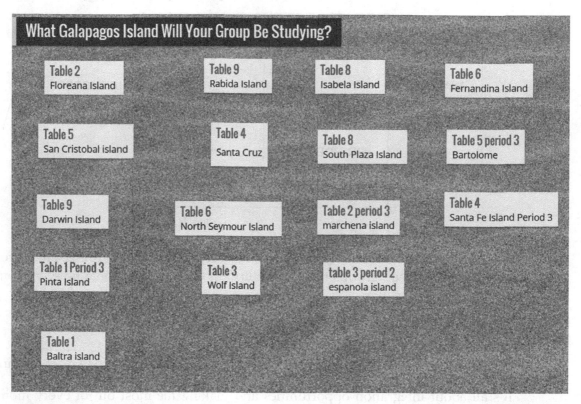

What Galapagos Island Will Your Group Be Studying?

Table 2 Floreana Island	**Table 9** Rabida Island	**Table 8** Isabela Island	**Table 6** Fernandina Island
Table 5 San Cristobal island	**Table 4** Santa Cruz	**Table 8** South Plaza Island	**Table 5 period 3** Bartolome
Table 9 Darwin Island	**Table 6** North Seymour Island	**Table 2 period 3** marchena island	**Table 4** Santa Fe Island Period 3
Table 1 Period 3 Pinta Island	**Table 3** Wolf Island	**table 3 period 2** espanola island	
Table 1 Baltra island			

5 **Collaboration Contract:** Set your students up for success by having their groups produce collaboration contract. By setting up expectations ahead of time, students can then design rubrics to assess their ability to collaborate at the end of the unit. See Part II for the collaboration contract assignment.

6 **Internet Literacy: Using Google Advanced Search:** As research begins, weave in different internet literacy lessons at the top of some research sessions and ask students to practice the skill of wiser searching. Requiring them to use Google Advanced Search is one step closer to better and more efficient searches. Look at Part II for the description of this lesson.

Homework Hint

Google screenshot: Have students provide you with a screenshot of the Google Advanced Search webpage, filled in with their specific search needs. They have to take a screen shot that proves they know how to get to the Google Advanced Search page and that they know what fields to fill in more specifically to have a more efficient search. This assignment is a credit/no credit activity (partial points given for late work, of course).

7 **Island Research:** In this lesson, have them use Google Advanced Search to learn more about the Galapagos Islands in order to understand more on the island on which they chose to focus their study.

Share a document with the students via Google Drive (or a single document for each group on which they can all add their notes prior to submission). This document is a template of questions and comments that they should divide up in order to research the islands of the Galapagos. Assuming there are four students for each group, each student should be responsible for researching at least two questions on the following template.

Galapagos Islands Research Template

1. What is the geography of the island?
2. What is the age of the island, and what are some ways scientists can predict this fact?
3. What is the location within the island chain? Take screenshot and embed it onto this document.
4. Using concrete description, describe the habitat of that island.
5. What species live there? Create a bulleted list of species' names.
6. What are the seasonal changes that might affect the species of this island?
7. On a scale of 1–10, 10 being rich with a variety of species, how abundant with species is your island? What number qualifies as a 1? As a 4? As a 7? As a 10?
8. Post an image of your island on the document.
9. Using MLA or APA format, cite your sources as you go and create a works cited page.

Tip on work accountability: In order to keep kids accountable for their own work when adding to a shared document, have each student select a different color font in which to write. Have the group create a key that tells you which color is assigned to which student, and ask those students to keep those colors throughout the course of the unit. In other words, yellow represents John's contributions in the collaboration notes as well as on the collaborative bibliography and the eventual executive summary. It makes grading a whole lot simpler if you start this from the beginning.

8 **Internet Literacy: Using Google News:** Teach students how to research the most up-to-date information by helping them use the Google search bar more effectively. For instance, you can specify that the Google gods only search a particular news outlet. If you type in, "news: National Geographic," you will notice that the only hits you then get are those found in *National Geographic*. Cool, right? Then begin to specify other elements to target. Use the drop-down menus below the search bar to make your searches even more specific. Specify how current news is or the format of the information: videos, images, websites, etc.

9 **Inquiry: Suggest Questions to Help Guide Their Research/Cornell Notes:** With the whole world open to them, it's important to provide guiding questions to students, at least at the beginning of a research project. After some momentum, however, you want to begin training them to develop questions themselves.

You can start with the following:

- ◆ What is a species?
- ◆ How do species get made?
- ◆ How many species need saving?
- ◆ Why are some species in danger?
- ◆ How are species saved?
- ◆ What happens to the ecosystem if a species disappears?
- ◆ Are some species more important than others?

Have them look specifically at a species on their selected island. Then, have them address the following:

- ◆ What other organisms is this species related to—how do you know this?
- ◆ Describe ways this species is specifically adapted to its environment and explain how these adaptations occurred.
- ◆ How did this species get to the islands—what evidence?
- ◆ What species in the fossil record is it related to? Cite evidence.
- ◆ What are people doing now to try and protect this species?
- ◆ Could this species survive on another island?

So, using Google Advanced Search, Instagrok, and Google News, you can have them begin to research the following about different or specific animals that are native to the Galapagos Islands:

- ◆ description
- ◆ habitat
- ◆ food
- ◆ reproduction
- ◆ numbers.

Have them use Cornell Notes to record their findings. A template for Cornell Notes can be found in Part II.

10 **Biodiversity Lesson:** Make sure you hit on explicit lesson(s) in biodiversity. Check out websites like www.crossingboundaries.org/ for inspiration in how to make this concept come alive through graphing, math prediction, and analysis.

11 **Punnett Square Assignment:** Help students predict the possible outcome of certain gene combinations using http://scienceprimer.com/punnett-square-calculator or other similar programs. Use the slide scale to show how probabilities are affected when certain gene combinations are introduced.

12 **Bring in an Expert from Outside the Classroom:** This is a good time to bring in an expert to help students continue their research so it isn't simply from website and print resources. In the case of the unit I developed, I offered up my mom to Skype into the classroom. She's a travel agent who specializes in eco-travel and had just returned from the Galapagos. Use any resource you have to find those people who have some connection to your unit. It can be a scientist, an artist who specializes in animal sketches, a taxidermist, whoever you can find by whatever means necessary.

Remember when you have a guest in the classroom to have students develop a list of norms for how to behave and be attentive for a guest speaker. Brainstorm as a class and then create a collaborative document that students can add to. Format this as a poster in the front of the room or as a handout by the door.

For example, one list my students created included the following:

1. Show respect. *(Note: I followed up on this suggestion with the question: What does respectful look like?)*
   ◆ Sit facing the speaker.
   ◆ Make eye contact and nod.
   ◆ Ask questions that follow up on what was said.
2. Laptops at 45 degrees if we aren't actively typing our notes.
3. Only use G-rated language (PG maybe).
4. Don't interrupt.
5. Use evidence, cite sources, and show your research when you ask questions.

13 **The Study of Extinction:** Begin to study extinction. What is it? How often does it happen? How does it affect the ecosystem in which it happens?

Homework Hint

Teams can throw together a "What if . . . ?" collaborative PowerPoint. Each student can create a slide that helps predict the ripple effect of a particular event's occurrence. For instance, what would have been the ripple effect if the T-Rex had not gone extinct? What will be the ripple effect if the bee does?

This kind of cause-and-effect prediction is found even in the elementary standards of the Common Core as:

CCSS.ELA-LITERACY.RI.3.3
Describe the relationship between a series of historical events, scientific ideas or concepts, or steps in technical procedures in a text, using language that pertains to time, sequence, and cause/effect.

Check out different resources besides simply those found online or in print. Watch an excerpt from Douglas Adams's *Last Chance to See*. This was a great documentary written by the author of *The Hitchhiker's Guide to the Galaxy* series where he went to see the last member of different species from around the world. It is also available in book form and is an amazing tribute to both the trials of eco-travel and those who devote their lives to saving these final creatures in a species.

Use Cornell Notes to take notes from the text or the video. A template on taking Cornell Notes can be found in Part II.

14 **Internet Literacy: Common Sense:** This is a good time to show them the "Save the Endangered Tree Octopus" website. This website uses Photoshop to create a site that supposedly is set up to raise money to save the dying tree octopus species in our great Northwest. However, click away and follow the links to find that it's really a false website with ties to Cafe Press. Fun stuff.

> ### Homework Hint
>
> Have the students write a journal entry that focuses on both empathy and extinction as they write from the POV of the last of a species.

15 **Species Design:** The key to real Project Based Learning isn't always about reporting out what exists, but in taking what you learn about what exists and creating your own version. In this case, once students conduct their research about their island and the various native animals in their location, they can then begin to imagine other species mythically adapted to their locale.

In other words, a habitat that might be ideal for a species like a crocodile might also prove ideal for a student-created species called the marine torguana (see Figure 3.4).

Figure 3.4 Student-Created Species

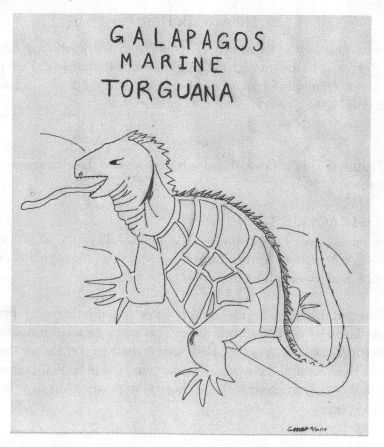

There are some fun programs out there for students to use to create new species. Try Build a Beast at http://animal.gamesxl.com/ or http://switchzoo.com/zoo.htm if students want to try a digital option.

Agreeing on what species to create might cause some bickering in the team, so make sure you work with them on building consensus and coming to decisions. To see my tips on building consensus, go to the Invention Unit chapter of this book.

16 **Digital Explorers' Journal:** Throughout this unit, once research has begun, students should begin chipping away at the creation of their exploration team's travel journal. This can be a physical journal, true, but it can also be in the form of a website (Weebly, Wix, or eMaze are cool) or multimedia presentation (PowerPoint, Google Presentation, Prezi, or Powtoons to name a few). Try to devote some time each day to work on this journal or divide up its components into homework assignments to help scaffold the overall production of the artifact.

The final explorers' journal should include the following information. Students can divide up the tasks and color code what they've done so that you, the teacher, can keep everyone accountable for their own contributions to the project.

◆ an image of the threatened species (the one they created);
◆ an image of the habitat in which the creature lives;
◆ a facts page about the island;
◆ facts about the animal;
◆ theories of why it is going extinct;
◆ Punnett Square and ratios/percentages;
◆ journal entries from the team's travel expedition and sketches of the environment, a la Darwin (for an interesting model of this, you might want to check out James Gurney's *Dinotopia*, a picture book in the costume of an explorer's journal that chronicles his travels to a mythical island where humans and dinosaurs coexisted; see the end of this chapter for an excerpt from a student's journal entry).

17 *Oral Presentation:* The explorers' journal becomes a piece of the oral presentation that will be presented, as a team, to the board of the Smithsonian in order to fund a species rescue of the created animal. The oral presentation must also include the following information:

◆ Research about the evolution of their mythical species.
◆ The "What if . . ." ripple effect if this species disappears.
◆ What we, as humans, can learn from the selected species.
◆ A "Save the (Animal Name)" persuasive campaign poster, webpage, or PSA (this can be a web page that resembles the one created for the tree octopus, a physical poster that can be used as a backdrop for the oral presentation, or even a video created on an iPad or Chromebook that is a mock commercial to help the species survive).
◆ A created plan for how this species could be best protected (specific, detailed recommendations; funding required; and technology needed).
◆ An infographic.

- ◆ Research library in MLA or APA bibliographic format.
- ◆ Practice the oral presentation first. Help students learn how to pace their oral presentation by giving them some guidance in timing themselves. Each presentation should last approximately 10 minutes tops, but that will take a little practice so the students aren't guessing how long their presentation will be. See a possible oral presentation timing sheet in Part II of this book.

As for scoring the oral presentations, you can use a quick and dirty rubric to assess the groups while still assigning individual scores. A rubric for quickly scoring individual oral presentations might look something like Table 3.2.

(18) Save the Species Selection: It would be ideal to bring in a scientist to hear the explorer team presentations and decide which group to fund. However, if the whole class role-plays as the board of the Smithsonian or the mythical World Animal Organization or something, that also "counts." You can also bring in members of your administration as well to be a part of the role-play and to help select the highest quality argument/content.

The board, whether made up of scientists, students, or admin, will be given X amount of (insert mythical organization's name) bucks to decide which of the groups' proposals to fund.

Table 3.2 Rubric for Individual Oral Presentations

	5	4	3	2	1
EYE CONTACT *Are you trapped in your notes, or are you connecting with your audience?*					
VOLUME *Can everyone hear you, even at the back of the room?*					
CONTENT *Is the information you are presenting clear and evidence based?*					
EMPHASIS *How well are you pronouncing the words? Are you speaking in a monotone, or are you more energized than that in your vocal range?*					
STANCE *Are you standing on your hip? Are your hands in your pockets or playing with your sleeve? Are you doing the middle school rock and roll?*					
SEAMLESSNESS *How well rehearsed is your group? Do you go from one part of your presentation to the other in a smooth way with practiced transitions? Have you tried all the technology you need to first to work out the problems ahead of time?*					
APPEARANCE *Are you dressed for success? No T-shirts allowed!*					

Tip on How to Assess Writing Quickly #3

Create feedback templates using a key of feedback symbols. Don't waste time writing in words. Create templates with the most common errors based on your subject, unit, assignment, etc. as a checklist of sorts to use from year to year. Make rubrics that can be circled or highlighted.

I personally love the Project Based Learning checklist website to create rubrics for easy scoring and feedback. You can explore it at http://pblchecklist.4teachers.org/.

Checklists may not be the most powerful strategy visually, but they're quick to produce, quick to fill out, and easy to read. Besides, if you mix this strategy up with others, kids will respond to the variety.

In the beginning of the year, identify the most common errors you predict you will see (or base it on their early work during the school year). Then develop a quick key of symbols or phrases you can use instead of writing in full sentences. When going through an assignment, you can quickly jot the symbol in the margin next to the error or check it off of a list, rather than writing out your comments for the student. You'll save time and energy, and this will require students to translate as well, which embeds the lesson even further.

I tend to create overall keys that reflect the most common writing errors and develop specific keys depending on the focus of a specific assignment. You can create a key of feedback symbols for any subject matter. Here is one I have used in the past:

———— Funky Wording

———— Run-On Sentence

———— Divide Ideas into Different Paragraphs

———— Fragment

———— Can't Read Your Writing Here

Student Exemplars

Student Exemplar

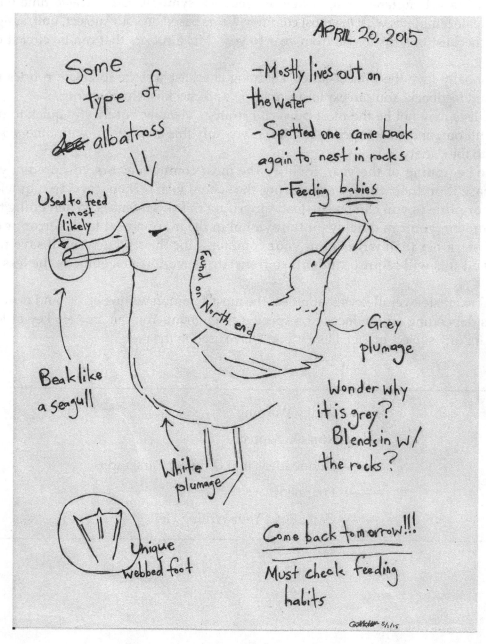

Hime Co.

HOME
FAQS
INFOGRAPHIC
RESEARCH
LIBRARY
THREATS
RESCUE
OPERATIONS

Save The Endangered Flyguana

Let It Soar Freely Once More!

RESCUE PLAN

First discovered in the 1970s, the Flyguana is a curios mix of an iguana and a bird, first discovered in the Galapagos Islands by scientist Yuta Pierre Horii. The full details of its evolution is unclear, but many researchers theorize that the Flyguana came from an iguana egg that hatched in the body of a bird. As a result of its incubation environment being the bird's stomach, the DNA from the bird mixed with the still unborn iguana. As a result, the Flyguana was born. This interesting creature, has a tail and head of an iguana, but has a body of a bird. It can grow up to a total of 22 centimeters of wingspan. It also has a number of different adaptations from its mixed DNA such as the bird's ability to fly, and the iguana's ability to climb. Sadly though, this amazing creature is endangered, with less than one thousand of its population left. To this extent, we, the Hime Company wish to ask for you aid in helping us save this species.

The Theme Park Unit

A Unit Based on the Engineering of Building a Theme Park Focused on
Mathematical Trial and Error and Various Thematic Genres

Table 4.1 Theme Park Unit Facts

Subjects Integrated	Physics—propulsion, energy, speed, motion, stability
	Additional science is based on student choice
	Math—area, perimeter, budgeting
	Writing—executive summary
	Reading—informational, biographies
	Technology—Google Drive, website design, internet literacy for research, presentations, hyperlinking, Roller Coaster Tycoon game
	Art—student choice (3D model, 2D blueprint, Minecraft model, etc.)
	Oral presentation
Skills Used	Collaboration
	Problem solving
	Creativity
	Communication
	Critical thinking
	Questioning
Duration	1 month
Driving Question	How can we entice the public to explore science?
Additional Advice Included	Tip on grading writing when you don't teach writing

Overview

The Theme Park Unit is one I initially designed for my language arts class. It centered on the creation of a theme park made up of lands centered on different reading genres. In this unit, I've switched out reading genres and built in lands based on different scientists and their contributions. Therefore, regardless of whether you teach physics, biology, or astronomy, you can theme the lands appropriate to your content area.

In this case, the students will be split into groups of four (more or less, depending on how many "lands" each theme park will have). Each student will research a different scientist from a different era and theme their land based on what they learn. Each land in the small group will combine together to become an entire theme park. Throughout the process, the students will learn not only about their individual scientist, but about the physics of roller coaster building. They will also budget the build of the park itself and write a pitch to a "board" convincing them to fund their vision. The unit ends with an oral presentation, complete with model, to this "board."

In the spirit of Project Based Learning, this unit will incorporate the following elements:

◆ writing
◆ experts in the classroom
◆ oral presentation
◆ role-play
◆ student choice
◆ problem solving
◆ collaboration
◆ real-world connections.

Because this unit was originally based in my language arts classroom, I have brought in an expert to help fill in some of the science content. Nevertheless, as with any PBL unit, you can pick and choose what will work with your lessons and what won't. Use the vehicle of the role-play (that of a theme park designer) to help propel the lessons you wish to convey.

Step-by-Step Lessons

I typically begin each unit with a checklist to help communicate the overarching goals of the unit. Because each lesson builds into the role-play of the unit, it's important to share with students and parents alike what's going on. Transparency is vital with PBL units because they can be very rigorous and not traditional. Therefore, some stakeholders don't recognize the learning unless they see how one lesson or assignments folds into the next. The following is a possible checklist to help pace your students through this unit.

Pacing Checklist

Date Assigned	Assignment	Deadline	Tardy?
	Entry event: video game		
	Selecting a scientist		
	Selecting biography on their scientist		
	Filling out scientist template		
	Annotating text		
	Collaboration constitution		
	Bringing an outside expert into the classroom		
	Theme park medium decision		
	Google Advanced Search		
	Research check		
	Bibliography uses MLA format http://owl.english.purdue.edu/owl/resource/560/01/ www.easybib.com/		

	The physics of roller coasters		
	Engineering vocab lesson using Kahoot		
	Math arch lesson		
	Prototyping the ride		
	Linking text		
	Creating infographics		
	Writing with numeracy		
	Budgeting template		
	Math of landscaping		
	Theme park ad and persuasive writing		
	Executive summary to board		
	Theme park presentation		
	Select theme park to be funded (extra points added to winning plan)		

Note that I have multiple columns that can be designated for different purposes. Some categories to choose from could be:

◆ date assigned
◆ assignment description
◆ due date
◆ days late
◆ resources to help you accomplish your goal
◆ deadline selected (if you are permitting students to commit to a choice of due dates).

Checklist

Welcome to the Theme Park Unit. You are role-playing as a theme park designer. You will be designing the coasters, landscaping the grounds, creating a budget, and pitching your kingdom to a board that will be making a decision about which theme park to fund.

You will be working with a small group of fellow designers, but each of you will be held accountable for your own contributions to the final theme park design and oral presentation.

I have included links as resources to help in your own independent learning. The expectation is that you are learning with me and despite me. You are learning with others and on your own. You are learning, but you are also teaching others. You are also expected to be your own advocate. Have questions? Freaking out? Talk to me. I'm your guide, and I'm here to help you achieve these goals to the best of your ability. I'm also here to push you to challenge what you think of as your best.

Attached is a rough checklist of assignments we will be chipping away at throughout the course of this unit.

Good luck, and reach out to me anytime.

1 **Entry Event: Video Game:** For this PBL unit, students are designing a new Six Flags theme park. They will be working in small groups wherein each student in the group will be designing both a roller coaster and a themed "land" that connects to other similarly created "lands." Get the students' brains a-spinnin' with an entry event that gets them thinking about both roller coasters and the layout of theme parks.

Introduce them to Roller Coaster Tycoon, a downloadable game for any computer platform. Play a few rounds with your students as a whole group activity, asking them simple questions like:

- What rides are in each land in a theme park?
- How many lands can make up an entire park?
- What fraction of the whole park does each land fill up?
- What equipment does each land need?
- What kind of landscaping does each land use?
- What other buildings help make up a land?
- What connects each ride?
- What connects each land?
- What are the similarities between each land?
- What are the differences?

Watch first-person perspectives of various roller coasters filmed with GoPros and other equipment. Check out http://wonderopolis.org/wonder/where-is-the-fastest-roller-coaster/ to get their brains primed to become roller coaster aficionados.

Each land will be based on a historic era, and the décor will be peppered with symbols and artifacts that reflect a particular scientist. Introduce the overall unit by filming an adult who is willing to role-play as a park owner looking for designers for a new Six Flags theme park. The students will be designing the following:

- a roller coaster;
- landscaping;
- placement of buildings (bathrooms, exits/entrances, gift shops, restaurants, etc.);
- pathways;
- anything else they can think of.

Here is a list of typical elements that my period 4 believed were present in every theme park:

- rides
- food/drink
- gift shops
- benches/places to gather
- bathrooms
- trash cans
- gates
- entrances/exits
- pathways
- lights
- grass
- roller coasters
- kiddie rides
- themes
- decorations
- decor

- ◆ employees
- ◆ mascots
- ◆ symbols
- ◆ janitors
- ◆ people working the rides
- ◆ maintenance people.

We brainstormed this list by using Padlet. Padlet is a digital bulletin board that allows students to throw ideas quickly onto the "board." You give the link to the board and they can quickly add thoughts to the public page.

Homework Hint

Have the students watch a YouTube clip of a patron's first-person perspective of a roller coaster ride. Have them sketch out what they think the ride looks like if the camera were pulled back to a more third-person perspective. They can bring the sketch in for simple homework points that can serve to help them brainstorm.

2 **Selecting a Scientist:** The first thing students have to do is select a scientist on whom to focus their research. The era in which this scientist existed serves as inspiration for the décor of the land each student will be designing. Each student gets to select a scientist based on his or her interests. Does a student like to study the stars? Maybe he or she can focus on Johann Bayer. Does a student have an interest in physics? Maybe that kid wants to dive into learning about Alhazen.

Of course, if you need to have some control over the kinds of scientists the students are selecting, you can always provide a list of representatives from that field and have a random draw.

3 **Selecting Biography on Their Scientist:** When producing any writing or presentation, it aids to have a parallel reading selections happening simultaneously. Not only will this help with research, but it will also help in supporting literacy school-wide.

It would further help to guide students in selecting a biography that is appropriate to their level and interests. Even if you don't teach reading per se, it's still helping create a net of literacy if you can also guide students in selecting a book that supports your content unit. To advise students on picking a book in your content area, you might want to ask them to do the following:

1. Look at the cover of the book. Does it look interesting?
2. Read the blurb or back of the book for a short summary.
3. Flip through the book and stop on a page. If it has more than five words the student doesn't know, then it might be too challenging for him/her to enjoy.
4. Encourage the student to read the hook of the book. Ask the student to read one to five pages to see if it gets the student involved in the story or information.
5. Read reviews on Amazon or the publisher's website. What have other people said about the book?

By helping students discover a book based on your content area, you are supporting literacy as well as your own subject matter area.

4 **Filling out Scientist Template:** As students conduct their research, they should be filling in a template that asks them to find answers to some basic questions about their scientist. They can unearth more facts, of course, but each student needs to come to the table at the end of their research with certain fundamental information.

It might look something like this:

> Name:
> Dates: (–)
> Field of study:
> Major contributions:
> Country of origin:
> Embed an image of the scientist.
> Embed an image of one or more of that scientist's discoveries, inventions, statements, etc.
> What is a symbol that might represent this person?

5 **Annotating Text:** As students read their biographies or print out any websites, have them annotate when they can. If they can write in the book, have them use the margins directly. If not, have them use post-its to stick to the pages they wish to annotate.

It's vital that science and math teachers teach annotation as well as their language arts and history counterparts. After all, if we want students to know how to read more informational or data-oriented text, they are better off having some guidance from you, their STEM-related educator.

But you don't have to do it alone. For tips on guiding students in how to annotate any genre of reading, look at the handout in Part II.

If you want students to annotate websites directly from their devices, you can use programs like Scrible that will permit students to add digital post-its and share resources to virtual bookshelves. If your students use iPads, Notability will permit them to annotate as well.

Most importantly, however, is to model the annotation you want the students to also use because interacting with the text will make the material "stick" much more effectively than simple reading. When reading an informational article, for instance, mark it up under the document camera or on the whiteboard. Narrate what your brain is doing while you are reading, jot it down in real time for students to see, and let the Think Aloud serve to model your support of all forms of literacy.

6 **Collaboration Constitution:** Before student groups can work successfully together, the small groups must develop norms for collaboration. To do this, they must create a collaboration constitution. This is a team charter of sorts, a contract that the students write as a group stating their expectations for each other. They focus on the duration of time that could reasonably pass before responding to an email, the progressive steps of their own ire if someone does not carry his or her own weight, and what those consequences might be after it gets to a certain point. They cover expectations on the frequency of working outside of school as well. All the group members then sign each document. The instructions for this assignment can be found in Part II.

Additionally, by the end of the unit overall, the groups can then also develop their own collaboration rubrics to assess each other on how well they worked together. The only catch is that they cannot include on the rubric an expectation that isn't specifically spelled out in the start-of-unit constitution. Student groups can design their rubrics for free using http://rubistar.4teachers.org.

A student example of a collaboration contract can be seen at the end of this chapter.

In fact, creating a contract of sorts between students who are being asked to work together fits nicely with a standard we see as early as primary school:

SL.1: Participate in collaborative conversations with diverse partners about grade 2 topics and texts with peers and adults in small and larger groups.

◆ Follow agreed-upon rules for discussions (e.g., gaining the floor in respectful ways, listening to others with care, speaking one at a time about the topics and texts under discussion).
◆ Build on others' talk in conversations by linking their comments to the remarks of others.
◆ Ask for clarification and further explanation as needed about the topics and texts under discussion.

7 Bringing an Outside Expert into the Classroom: As with many PBL units, try to bring in an expert from outside the classroom. Of course, there are tons of wonderful online archives and resources out there from which to learn, but if you are able to bring in a designer, a landscaper, an "Imagineer," or an architect, make sure you go over your norms for having a guest speaker in the classroom. Even if you have someone Skype into the classroom, make sure you go over norms. A handout of videoconferencing norms can be found in Part II of this book.

In addition, helping students prepare to conduct an interview is also an important part of the frontloading process. To help guide students in conducting an interview, whether in the classroom or outside of the classroom, provide them with the handout "How to Conduct an Interview" in Part II of this book.

8 Theme Park Medium Decision: As students begin to research and design their theme parks and the lands that make up each park, the groups are bound to have to make decisions that require them to come to a consensus. Figuring out the medium in which they will construct their theme park is one of them. One student might want to build it digitally using Minecraft. Another might want to build the theme park out of Legos. The fact is that the one decision they must all agree on eventually is how to physically create the theme park they will be presenting to possible investors.

Guide students by giving them options in how to make those decisions. To learn more about guiding students to reach a consensus, check out the Invention Unit earlier in this book.

9 Google Advanced Search: Teaching internet literacy skills is vital when asking students to research online, and a simple way to begin is in teaching students how to use Google Advanced Search.

1. First, have students go to Google Search (the regular homepage) and type in their keywords or questions to begin their research.
2. Have them mark the number of hits that appeared using their method.
3. Then show students how to access Google Advanced Search and require them to explore some of its customization features.
4. Then have them record the number of hits based on a more detailed Google Advanced Search.
5. Have them print out a screenshot of the customized Google screenshot and mark their initial hit number and revised hit number somewhere on the page.

See Part II for an activity focusing on this concept.

Homework Hint

Have students provide you with a screenshot of the Google Advanced Search web page, filled in with their specific search needs. They have to take a screen shot that proves they know how to get to the Google Advanced Search page and that they know what fields to fill in more specifically to have a more efficient search. Voila! Instant credit/no credit assignment (partial points given for late work, of course).

10 **Research Check:** A possible quiz assignment is to check the students' ongoing research by having research checks. These checks are a quick look at a growing list of bibliographical resources that students will be using to seed the science into their theme parks. Their lists should be alphabetized and should use proper MLA format. Furthermore, at the end of the unit, these bibliography lists should also correlate to the hyperlinks in any written work as well as with the citations at the end of their executive summaries.

11 **The Physics of Roller Coasters:** Elements of these lessons were shared with me by two wonderful educators, Emily Cruz and Melanie Valencia. These two teachers brought their individual educator super powers to a rich roller coaster design unit that asked their elementary students to participate in a flipped classroom model. Cruz says that "students watched videos (flipped model) and come to class prepared to put that knowledge to work."

Their unit combined digital trial and error with offline experimentation. They used writing and science with their students and, as a result, guided elementary students toward understanding complex concepts in physics.

Some resources they used to help their elementary students understand the concepts of roller coaster physics were:

Newton's Law of Motion

YouTube, Newton's 3 (Three) Laws of Motion:
www.youtube.com/watch?v=mn34mnnDnKU&feature=youtu.be

Force and Kinetic Energy

YouTube, Kinetic and Potential Energy:
www.youtube.com/watch?v=vl4g7T5gw1M&feature=youtu.be

Easy Science for Kids, All about Force: Push and Pull:
   http://easyscienceforkids.com/all-about-force-push-and-pull/
Scholastic StudyJams, Force & Motion:
   http://studyjams.scholastic.com/studyjams/jams/science/forces-and-motion/
   force-and-motion.htm

Potential Energy

BrainPOP, Potential Energy:
   www.brainpop.com/science/energy/potentialenergy/preview.weml

---

Homework Hint

Have students look at the designs of Rube Goldberg. Have them go to www.rubegoldberg.com/ or check out YouTube videos people have made in honor of Goldberg's work. Now, while we aren't necessarily asking students to develop a machine for this unit, it is important that they understand sequence and procedure. Have students select a machine and break it down into its components, identifying each step either through writing or visual note taking. It might just help students see the components that make up a roller coaster ride.

---

12 **Engineering Vocab Lesson Using Kahoot:** Kahoot is a fun online tool that allows teachers to gamify simple question/response activities. Create something using Kahoot that focuses on simple vocabulary to help students acquire a common language for the physics being use in the classroom.

Words that help define simple machines are important to begin seeping into the classroom. Try to help students learn those words, but gamify their lessons. Help them learn simple concepts like:

   ◆ wedge
   ◆ pulley
   ◆ wheel and axle
   ◆ lever
   ◆ screw
   ◆ inclined plane.

Check out www.teachengineering.org/ for lessons and concepts that will help students understand simple machines and how they work.

13 **Math Arch Lesson:** Use a program like the one provided at www.desmos.com/calculator to have the students create an arch. Have them fool around with the variables so they can see what happens to their arch if the math is adjusted in any way.

14 **Prototyping the Ride:** It's valuable for students to be able to prototype the ride upon which they are focusing many of their physics lessons. Have them look at different videos of 3D models or even look at this video from Quirky.com that has blossoming inventors create prototypes out of cardboard. You can find it at www.quirky.com/blog/post/2014/12/cardboard-prototype.

Of course, you can use programs like FossWeb to digitally prototype your roller coasters, but anything that makes the students' ideas more concrete is bound to help with the quality in the end of the unit.

Elementary teacher Emily Cruz says the following about the importance of prototyping in her roller coaster physics unit:

> Students use foam tubing, marbles, and tape to construct their coasters. Each day, the groups focus on a different component (curve, hill, loop). As students work to successfully design each component, the teacher walks around to conference with students about the forces and motion at play. Students document each trial in their notebooks, giving reasons why they worked or didn't work, using the vocabulary from the videos. Students draw and take pictures to collect data. Once they have a successful trial, students use the iPads to take a picture of the coaster. Students use an annotating app (such as Skitch) to label the parts of the coaster, document measurements, and identify potential and kinetic energy (or other concepts of forces and motion).

You can see photos of Emily's students at the end of this unit.

15 **Linking Text:** Teach students about hyperlinking. Hyperlinking is when the writer creates another, more transparent, level of their writing by linking keywords to their research. For instance, if a student writes that her main roller coaster contains an inverted loop, she might link the keywords "inverted loop" to the Coaster Force website article on various kinds of inversions, thus proving some kind of layer of research beyond the mere defined writing.

16 **Creating Infographics:** It's important to have students understand that text, numbers, and pictures have a relationship. Infographics not only blend them all, but also help integrate subjects. For this unit, students can design infographics about everything from the science their theme park represents to basic information on the "land," communicating the costs and the predicted earnings from the developed park should it be funded. They should include their infographics in their final presentations as evidence of fact-based persuasion. To create infographics, I introduce them to piktochart.com as a great infographic-producing program, but I permit students to use any program to design their infographics so long as they include all the elements. A lesson to introduce students to analyzing and creating infographics can be found in Part II of this book.

See the end of this chapter for a student sample on world hunger.

Homework Hint

Once you have introduced infographics to the students, have them find examples in the world outside of school and bring them in for credit. They can see for themselves that they need to understand how to read them if they begin to realize just how many are out there and how many subjects they represent.

17 **Writing with Numeracy:** We talk a lot about students needing to embed evidence into their writing, but are we specifically teaching how to write using numbers? To counter what I felt was a gap in my own practice, I researched how mathematicians and scientists and those in higher education were solving this problem. I found a handful of rules many of them follow (and a few that were specific to particular content areas). I combined them into a reference sheet for students and tacked on a few questions for them to answer that forced them to interact and refer to the cheat sheet I'd created. You can see it in Part II.

In the case of the theme park unit, the students are eventually going to be combining their knowledge of physics with a pitch letter/executive summary that will undoubtedly include some kind of data, statistics, and numbers that need to be embedded organically into the writing. It's important, therefore, to provide students with some kind of guidance in how to write using numbers.

18 **Budgeting Template:** Have the students use something like Excel or Google Spreadsheets to create an itemized budget of predicted costs to build their theme park land. Their price points can come from research of similar projects. Help brainstorm a list of searchable terms and tags that students can research. Have them develop those terms into questions to help them build their inquiry skills. For instance:

Terms

- theme park
- development costs
- attendance
- construction

Possible Question Developed

- What are the development costs to construct a new theme park, and how many visitors must attend per year to break even?

19 **Math of Landscaping:** Conduct an area and perimeter lesson that helps students develop the blueprints for the landscaping of their lands. Have them make decisions about the following:

- How long are the paths from attraction to attraction?
- Where are the shrubs, and how much space will they occupy along those paths?
- How much area will the center of your land occupy?
- Will there be a circular fountain or an octagonal one? How much space will this occupy?
- How much grass will need to be planted in the picnic zone beside your themed restaurant?

Have students brainstorm the flora and fauna beforehand and then use SketchUp to design the visuals in a digital blueprint.

This kind of real world use of area and perimeter is seen in the third grade Common Core Standards:

CCSS.MATH.CONTENT.3.G.A.2
Partition shapes into parts with equal areas. Express the area of each part as a unit fraction of the whole.

And it also appears all through the grades on up through high school:

High School: Use coordinates to compute perimeters of polygons and areas of triangles and rectangles, e.g., using the distance formula.

20 **Theme Park Ad and Persuasive Writing:** Have students develop a persuasive advertisement to market the opening of their theme park. Study the old Disneyland posters that featured particular rides or have them look at Six Flags websites for ideas on how to get ticket buyers through their gates. Develop a possible rubric for these ads that could instruct students in the following:

◆ uses persuasive words;
◆ pitches the ticket price;
◆ features a particular ride;
◆ identifies traits about the ride that make it awesome;
◆ includes an image of the ride;
◆ includes a background of the décor of the land;
◆ is written in a font that reflects STEM.

Teaching about how to pitch any content area is not only real world and authentic writing, but it also helps support the efforts of the ELA teachers and their task to teach persuasive writing. As it says in the standards:

Grade 8: Write arguments to support claims with clear reasons and relevant evidence

After all, an ad that incorporates persuasive word choice is, indeed, another genre of writing.

21 **Executive Summary to Board:** The end of the unit culminates in an oral presentation based on a formally written executive summary. The purpose of an executive summary is to pitch a concept to a busy person by using a simple structure and subheadings to break up the ideas within. Each student should be responsible to write his or her own executive summary based on the research for their "land."

The outline of a typical executive summary can be found in Part II. However, rather than break down their subheadings into Background, Evidence, and Recommendations, have those terms instead reflect engineering nomenclature. To align an executive summary used in an ELA class with engineering terms, I looked to an open source MIT class. I found a term, BIRAC, that can be used to mirror the sections used in a typical executive summary. For the purposes of this written pitch to a mythical board, convert the standard executive summary subheadings into engineering-aligned ones such as the following:

B—Background: Define the plan by posing a question.
I—Issues: What can you predict might limit what you hope to happen?
R—Recommendations: What methods do you suggest in how to proceed with your plans?
A—Analysis: What evidence and analysis proves your recommendation has some merit?
C—Consequences: What are the consequences of rejecting or accepting your suggestions?

So, in other words, a theme park executive summary using engineering terminology might break down into the following:

B—Background

How can the city provide a place for families to go that might entice children, teens, and adults in a safe environment? Can this proposed location also bring money into the city coffers?

I—Issues

It's possible that the terrain will be tricky to work with. Also, we would need to convince the neighbors of the selected area to live with the construction and traffic that would increase during the build and after its completion.

R—Recommendations

We suggest that we build a theme park in order to bring a family-friendly environment to our city.

A—Analysis

The evidence might include: traffic pattern predications, cost analysis to build, predicted ticket-buying income, research about similar projects conducted in the past, etc.

C—Consequences

This will be based on the facts from the analysis and predictions of what might be earned and lost if the said contract is not adopted.

For the purposes of this unit, the executive summary essay has to include the following:

- different text structures;
- hyperlinks;
- a claim;
- cited textual evidence from a variety of resources;
- background information on the research it took to formulate the theme park plan;
- how the elements of the theme park relate to science;
- a call to action that is concrete and specific;
- a logical prediction of the cost to build the park and the possible earnings that can be brought in from sales.

22 **Theme Park Presentation:** The real culmination of this unit is in the oral presentation that will be given to a "board" of theme park executives. OK, so maybe it's just the class, but you can always supplement students with people outside of the classroom to bring in a more authentic audience. Invite the local Board of Education or perhaps an architect or two. You can even bring in a landscape designer, set designer, or physics expert. The key is to bring in someone who might have some stake in the precision of the students' information.

The final presentation should reflect the work of the whole group. Each student in the group should be presenting three to five slides on their specific "land." They must go into detail about their assigned scientist, the science used in their roller coaster design, and the layout of their "land," as well as any decisions they made regarding their décor and landscaping. Each student is also in charge of providing a piece to an itemized spreadsheet that will be a collaborative document that reflects the cost to build the whole theme park in its entirety.

In addition, there should be a component that displays the whole visual of the combined lands. That is, there should be a layout of the whole theme park itself. This could be a sketched eagle's-eye view from overhead of the whole park (a la a Disneyland map) or a 3D tour through a Minecraft realm. It can be made from Legos or a poster that was assembled like a puzzle, combining people's lands all together. Regardless, the students need to show that their concepts, however unique, all fit together into one collaborative project.

After all, we can see this kind of expectation set up in the following standard:

> W.6: With guidance and support from adults, use a variety of digital tools to produce and publish writing, including in collaboration with peers.

You can find a generic rubric for oral presentations in Part II of this book.

23 **Select Theme Park to Be Funded:** Have students (or outside stakeholders who viewed the presentations) vote on the best presentation in their classroom. These teams will have their theme park on display somewhere in the main office or in a local establishment to indicate that their theme park design was "selected" for construction.

✎ Tip on How to Assess Writing Quickly #4

Comment rather than correct. Carol Jago says we should "comment rather than correct," and she's dead right. It should be the students' job to correct their errors, but it's our job to make them think about what those errors could possibly be.

Therefore, create questions as a means to have them look deeper. If you don't spell it out for them, they eventually won't be coming to you so often for the quick answers. Developing questions will help guide them to become better problem solvers, and that's a skill that will help them in the future.

In fact, you can make your feedback a scavenger hunt of sorts by using some of the following sentence stems:

In your essay, I see (*general mistake*) appear X amount of times.
In your lab report, I see two errors in your hypothesis statements.
In your math assignment, I see three equations that do not add up.

Remember, you want them to be paying attention to your advice. Keep them awake and alert to your guidance by making them work for it.

Student Exemplars

Theme Park Design Team

Collaboration Contract

Our four "lands" (and their individual contractors) are as follows:

Teslaville: The Electric Domain!—Matthew
Einsteinia: Land of Motion—William
Goodall-Land: Place of Chimps & Biology—Dylan
Rock World: The World of Rocks—Raymond

Overall Rules:

- ◆ We will always communicate at school during 4th period.
- ◆ We will also use Skype to communicate after school hours.
- ◆ All of the League members are required to meet after school on Fridays every week at the Media Center, 3:00–3:30 or to 4:00.
- ◆ All of the League members must reply to a message within 3 hours or less.
- ◆ We will hit all deadlines in order for the group elements of our project to proceed on time.

Problem Solving:

- ◆ We will have a group conference if one does not do their fair share or participate. Participate or fail, we will not allow the member that isn't cooperating to receive credit of the work.
- ◆ All of the League members must problem solve their problems before asking the teacher for intervention. Discussing the problem is the first step to problem solving.

Group Responsibilities in Addition to Individual Assignments:

Matthew will be the timer, and will keep records of our meetings and accomplishments.
William is the group leader and may ask questions of teacher or other collaborative groups as the representative of our organization.
Dylan is the key researcher and will go through our evidence and Works Cited to verify facts.
Raymond is the overall continuity designer. He will ensure that the visuals and the writing all coincide and coordinate.

Norms of Our Theme Park Team:

- ◆ Everyone has to contribute in some way.
- ◆ Treat everyone with kindness and respect.
- ◆ Everyone is supposed to be on time and prepared for their tasks daily.
- ◆ Help each other.

- ◆ Celebrate success when we finish our given task.
- ◆ Everyone is treated equally.
- ◆ Everyone is special in their very own way.
- ◆ Always try your best, no matter if things seem tough.
- ◆ He who does not work, neither shall he earn an A.
- ◆ Working will earn rewards while slacking off will earn punishments.
- ◆ Always have all of your materials ready for every task.
- ◆ Complete all tasks before starting a new one.

Mission Statement:

The objective of our Theme Park team is to work together as a group, in order to develop the artifact we intend. We will use our unique and special skills to assist each other, and we will accept and listen to the rules and norms of our constitution in order to complete our goals. No one will be left behind; everyone will be treated equally and fairly.

By signing this constitution, all team members will pledge to follow these rules/ideas and help those in need.

_____   _____   _____   _____
Matthew   William   Dylan   Raymond

Student Exemplar

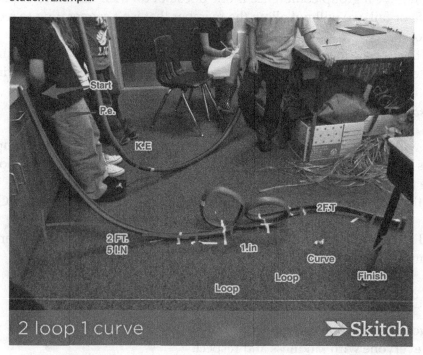

2 loop 1 curve   ➤ Skitch

Student Exemplar

Student Exemplar

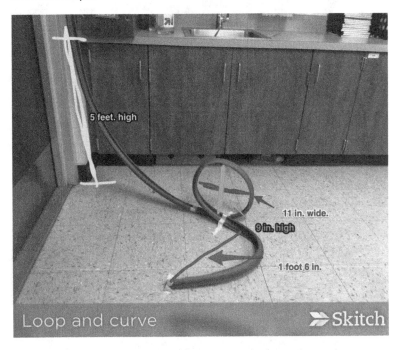

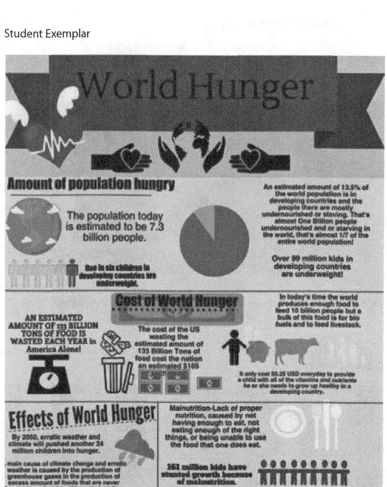

World Hunger

Amount of population hungry

The population today is estimated to be 7.3 billion people.

An estimated amount of 13.5% of the world population is in developing countries and the people there are mostly undernourished or staving. That's almost One Billion people undernourished and or starving in the world, that's almost 1/7 of the entire world population!

Over 99 million kids in developing countries are underweight!

One in six children in developing countries are underweight.

Cost of World Hunger

AN ESTIMATED AMOUNT OF 133 BILLION TONS OF FOOD IS WASTED EACH YEAR in America Alone!

The cost of the US wasting the estimated amount of 133 Billion Tons of food cost the nation an estimated $165

In today's time the world produces enough food to feed 10 billion people but a bulk of this food is for bio fuels and to feed livestock.

It only cost $0.25 USD everyday to provide a child with all of the vitamins and nutrients he or she needs to grow up healthy in a developing country.

Effects of World Hunger

By 2050, erratic weather and climate will pushed another 24 million children into hunger.

main cause of climate change and erratic weather is caused by the production of greenhouse gases in the production of excess amount of foods that are never been eaten when bought, wasted, and or for other purposes.

World Hunger could be solved right now, but because of corporate goals, poverty, and inequality the problem isn't solved yet. Everyone can band together to help end world hunger, it will take time and lots of resources, but it can be done and save millions.

Malnutrition-Lack of proper nutrition, caused by not having enough to eat, not eating enough of the right things, or being unable to use the food that one does eat.

161 million kids have stunted growth because of malnutrition.

Did you know that hunger kills more people each year than AIDS, Malaria, and Tuberculosis combined?

Poor nutrition causes nearly half (45%) of deaths in children under five - 3.1 million children each year.

Malnutrition can cause increase of death chance, diet related diseases, and health conditions.

Works Cited

"2013 World Hunger and Poverty Facts and Statistics by World Hunger Education Service." 2013 World Hunger and Poverty Facts and Statistics by World Hunger Education Service. Web. 11 Dec. 2014. <http://www.worldhunger.org/articles/Learn/world hunger facts 2002.htm>.

"About Global Hunger." Bread. Web. 11 Dec. 2014. <http://www.bread.org/hunger/global/>.

"Malnutrition: MedlinePlus Medical Encyclopedia." U.S National Library of Medicine. U.S. National Library of Medicine. Web. 11 Dec. 2014. <http://www.nlm.nih.gov/medlineplus/ency/article/000404.htm>.

"We Already Grow Enough Food for 10 Billion People... and Still Can't End Hunger." Common Dreams. Web. 11 Dec. 2014. <http://www.commondreams.org/views/2012/05/08/we-already-grow-enough-food-10-billion-people-and-still-cant-end-hunger>.

"World Food Programme Fighting Hunger Worldwide." Hunger. Web. 11 Dec. 2014. <http://www.wfp.org/hunger>.

"World Food Programme Fighting Hunger Worldwide." Hunger Statistics. Web. 11 Dec. 2014. <http://www.wfp.org/hunger/stats>.

"World Food Programme Fighting Hunger Worldwide." What Is Malnutrition? Web. 11 Dec. 2014. <http://www.wfp.org/hunger/malnutrition>.

"Stop Hunger Now." Stop Hunger Now. Web. 18 Nov. 2014. <http://www.stophungernow.org/hunger-facts>.

"World Hunger Facts." Freedom from Hunger. Web. 18 Nov. 2014. <https://www.freedomfromhunger.org/world-hunger-facts>.

The Teach Them to Be Teachers Unit

A Unit Based on the Highest Level of Communication of All . . . the Ability to Teach

Table 5.1 Teach Them to Be Teachers Unit Facts

Subjects Integrated	Writing—informational plan, persuasive business letter
	Reading—informational
	Technology—Google Drive, internet literacy for research, Google Forms, Google Spreadsheets, multiple intelligences vs. learning styles
	All subjects—depending on the topic selected by the student, a particular student might focus on a science-related subject, a history-related subject, an athletic subject, etc.
Skills Used	Creativity
	Communication
	Critical thinking
	Oral presentation
	Independent learning
	Reciprocal teaching
	Peer teaching
Duration	2 weeks to 1 month
Driving Question	What are the skills needed to teach others?

Overview

In my book, *'Tween Crayons and Curfews: Tips for Middle School Teachers*, I devote an entire chapter to the rationale of why we must teach our students to be master communicators. That is, I make an argument for why we must teach our students to be teachers. I say the following:

> If what Aristotle says is true, that "Teaching is the highest form of understanding," then should not the "Ability to Teach" be our highest form of praise for a student? After all,

when we assess students, what are we really asking them to do? We're requiring that they prove content knowledge and the ability to communicate that knowledge. Is that not teaching in its purest form?

Think about the skills a teacher needs to do his or her job. Here's a partial list:

◆ communication
◆ research skills
◆ problem solving
◆ setting rigorous expectations
◆ giving feedback.

These are the skills of not only a teacher, but of a leader, of a group member, and of a key player. These are the skills that students will use in their own futures. Someone once said that "Teaching is the profession that teaches all the other professions," so why not sow the seed of teaching early on?

The final chapter in Part I of this book takes this rationale a step further by providing step-by-step lessons through my Teach the Teacher PBL unit. In it, students are guided to select an activity for which they have some modicum of knowledge and a great deal of passion. It can be a specific topic or even a skill. They must then teach their peers about this interest and then pitch it as a possible future elective to an administrator.

This unit incorporates the following PBL elements:

◆ role-play
◆ authentic audience
◆ peer teaching
◆ student-created resources
◆ oral presentation
◆ student choice.

Try this unit, or its scaffolds, to highlight any subject area. The cool thing about this unit is that you can give students as much structure as you want while still giving them choice. Full freedom of topic will certainly earn you some interesting lessons! If you want to focus their topics, however, on historical topics or scientific topics, that would allow you some control over content while still granting them choice.

As I say in my past book:

Students must be taught to teach. They must learn to teach each other, and in so doing, will learn to teach themselves. After all, education's job is not to always be there for the student, but to give them the skills to be their own source of education during their life. What a tragic classroom it would be if the students always remain the pupils.

Step-by-Step Lessons

Pacing Checklist

Date Assigned	Assignment	How to Submit
	Finding a topic (dual-entry journal)	
	Problem statement	
	Bibliography check	
	Google Advanced Search	
	The six steps of being an internet detective	
	Using Wikipedia wisely	
	Multiple intelligences quiz results	
	Lesson plan	
	Developing an assessment	
	Student-created rubric	
	Oral presentation timing sheet	
	Visual for oral presentation	
	Oral presentation	
	Backchanneling questions	
	Administering, scoring, and analyzing scored quiz responses	
	Persuasive letter to administrator	

1 Finding a Topic (Dual-Entry Journal): The whole focus of this unit is student choice, but as we know, without guidance, students can sometimes select topics that are beneath their abilities. So give them some structure in finding their topic. That way, you've at least had them think ahead before committing to something too challenging or too easy.

Have the students list three possible topics and create a dual-entry journal that explores the pros and cons of each. They might want to think about the "history of . . ." a topic or perhaps a "how to . . ." kind of skill. A template might look like this:

Possible Topic #1

Pros	Cons
◆	◆
◆	◆
◆	◆

Possible Topic #2

Pros	Cons
◆	◆
◆	◆
◆	◆

Possible Topic #3

Pros	Cons
◆	◆
◆	◆
◆	◆

Some fun topics that students have wanted to teach are as follows:

- How to solve a Rubik's Cube
- The history of the Los Angeles Lakers
- How to make my nana's famous enchiladas
- How to succeed at *Guitar Hero*
- The history of skateboarding
- The science of earthquakes
- How to read a sonnet.

Now, this unit is a great end-of-year unit that can embrace student choice fully, allowing kids to decide on the topic that is most interesting to them and one in which they already have expertise. It can reflect their hobbies and likes. However, it can also be used to reflect on what's been learned during the school year under your tutelage.

To use this unit toward that purpose, brainstorm a list of topics, skills, and/or standards that have been covered throughout the school year and use this unit as a means to embed them further before saying good-bye to the school year.

And how 'bout this one: you can also go one step further and assign students standards or topics from next year's curriculum and see what they can accomplish independently to frontload learning before they leave your room for the last time.

Depending on the topic selected, different standards will be hit by each student. You may have a student presenting on how to use a mathematical equation to solve a Rubik's Cube. That being the case, the student might discover this hits the following Common Core Standards:

High School Algebra: Rearrange formulas to highlight a quantity of interest, using the same reasoning as in solving equations.

6th Grade Algebra: Find the volume of a right rectangular prism with fractional edge lengths by packing it with unit cubes of the appropriate unit fraction edge lengths, and show that the volume is the same as would be found by multiplying the edge lengths of the prism.

Grade 3: Solve real world and mathematical problems involving perimeters of polygons, including finding the perimeter given the side lengths, finding an unknown side length, and exhibiting rectangles with the same perimeter and different areas or with the same area and different perimeters.

The list if standards hit can go on and on . . .

2 **Problem Statement:** The problem statement is a formal document that is intended to prove a certain level of knowledge in order to pitch the topic to the teacher. If a student selects a high-level topic, but hasn't conducted some basic, fundamental research in order to construct a problem statement, the teacher knows right away the topic will not work for that student. Conversely, even the silliest of topics can be made more rigorous by first requiring a problem statement be constructed at the top of the unit.

The format of a problem statement is as follows:

◆ A student must construct a short two- to three-paragraph informational overview of a topic that they believe they may want to research further.

◆ It also includes three to five questions about the topic that can guide future research. The questions can even be used for Google searches if needed.

The handout to construct a problem statement and a higher-level example can be found in Part II of this book. You can see student samples from a Teach the Teacher unit at the end of this chapter.

Regardless of the unit in which it is used, constructing a problem statement hits individualized math and science standards, to be sure. However, it also supports the overall literacy and writing standards that all classes must now be responsible to teach. So, in addition to your content standards, having students construct problem statements also hit the following Common Core Standards:

CCSS.ELA-LITERACY.W.8.1.A
Introduce claim(s), acknowledge and distinguish the claim(s) from alternate or opposing claims, and organize the reasons and evidence logically.

CCSS.ELA-LITERACY.W.8.1.B
Support claim(s) with logical reasoning and relevant evidence, using accurate, credible sources and demonstrating an understanding of the topic or text.

CCSS.ELA-LITERACY.W.8.7
Conduct short research projects to answer a question (including a self-generated question), drawing on several sources and generating additional related, focused questions that allow for multiple avenues of exploration.

3 **Bibliography Check:** The students need to focus on specific and rigorous research, especially if the topic they've selected (and you've approved) is a less rigorous one. Therefore, it's important that while the unit itself may be untraditional, the research you require should have a structure that has higher expectations. That's where teaching about bibliographical format comes in. Having said that, I still encourage independent learning by having the students access the resources that help teach them proper MLA or APA format.

The first thing I do is provide students the link to the Purdue Online Writing Lab and, more specifically, to the general guidelines for web-based resources. I point the way to https://owl.english.purdue.edu/owl/resource/560/01, but they then repeatedly access the resource as needed.

I'd be lying if I said that I showed them the proper way to cite major resources when, in fact, it's EasyBib that does that. Frankly, it's Google Drive that does it. As an add-on from Drive, EasyBib allows students to plug in key information, and then the program formats it and adds it as a works cited page. It's pretty darn cool. As soon as I show them how easy it is, citing work becomes a requirement for every submitted assignment. No excuses when so much is done for you digitally, right?

4 **Google Advanced Search:** See Part II in this book for more on this lesson. This is an easy assignment, not only to require, but also to score.

1. First, have students go to Google Search (the regular homepage) and type in their keywords or questions to begin their research.
2. Have them mark the number of hits that appeared using their method.
3. Then show students how to access Google Advanced Search and require them to explore some of its customization features.
4. Then have them search again, recording the revised number of hits based on a more detailed Google Advanced Search.
5. Have them print out a screenshot of the customized Google screenshot and mark their initial hit number and revised hit number somewhere on the page.

Voila! Instant credit/no credit assignment.

5 **The Six Steps of Being an Internet Detective:** Talk to students about the different ways they can look at websites with a critical eye. For instance, teach them the literacy of reading URL extensions. What's the difference between .edu and .gov? Teach them that links are telling. If you click on links, where do they take you? Check out the handout in Part II of this book for a list of the Six Steps of Being an Internet Detective.

6 **Using Wikipedia Wisely:** Here's a simple activity that helps students utilize one of the most widely used research entry points out there: Wikipedia. I am not anti-Wikipedia. I do, however, feel that I need to teach students how to use Wikipedia. I've spoken to people at CalTech, MIT, Harvard, etc. Everyone, at some point, has used Wikipedia as a jumping-off point. But we have to teach kids how to use it skeptically. To address this need, I have developed a quick four-part activity.

Step 1: Go to Wikipedia and type in your topic. For the purposes of this example, let's use Nikola Tesla (see Figure 5.1). Read the entry to think about an interesting fact that you might have learned, but question it. Is it really true, or is it a Wikipedia myth?

Step 2: Pull out keywords, dates, or proper nouns that help identify an interesting fact about the topic. In this case, I'm interested to confirm if Tesla really did work for Thomas Edison, so I'm pulling out the following:

Tesla, Edison, 1884, New York

Step 3: Convert those keywords into a question that you can then use for the search function in Google.

Step 4: Analyze the first page of the Google Search based on the question you asked. You will pull up a list of hits on Google, and on the first page alone, you will most likely see that multiple websites that aren't Wikipedia seem to validate the fact being researched. And if multiple websites can confirm it right there in the summaries on the Google page, there's a great chance that Wikipedia reported this one fact reliably.

You can also use my Internet Literacy: Verifying the Evidence Lesson (in Part II of this book) on how to verify the evidence on a website to continue encouraging inquiry as a means to promote further research.

Figure 5.1 Wikipedia Search

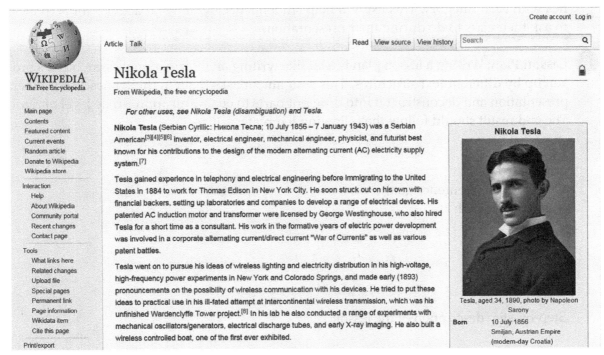

Source: https://en.wikipedia.org/?title=Nikola_Tesla

> ## Homework Hint
>
> *Bibliography Research Check:* Do quick checks of the growing list of resources each student should be gathering on his or her topic. Grades can be issued based on proper formatting as well as quality of resources. I only permit students to use Wikipedia once on these lists. It gives them a good jumping-off place but shouldn't define their research. No About.com, eHow.com, or Ask.com allowed!

Besides teaching internet literacy because it's a logical lesson in efficient research skills, the Common Core Standards also requires it:

CCSS.ELA-LITERACY.W.8.8
Gather relevant information from multiple print and digital sources, using search terms effectively; assess the credibility and accuracy of each source; and quote or paraphrase the data and conclusions of others while avoiding plagiarism and following a standard format for citation.

7 Multiple Intelligences Quiz Results: Have students learn a bit about the concept of multiple intelligences. This is not so that they can learn about their own, however. It's more to acknowledge that other intelligences exist in the room that they need to understand if they are to successfully teach the teacher and their peers.

Have them go to www.edutopia.org/multiple-intelligences-assessment and take the 24-question quiz to determine their own category. Then have them click on each of the intelligences listed at the end of their assessment to discover more about what it means to have those strengths and tendencies.

Have students brainstorm different activities that might engage a learner who identi-fies with each category. This list will help students decide on what activity (or activities) to ask their class to do during their presentation.

8 **Lesson Plan:** Writing a lesson plan is a lot like writing an informational essay, but it's bro-ken up by different text structures. This assignment asks them to think ahead about their presentation and deconstruct it into different parts to ensure an appropriate level of rigor. The end result should follow the following template:

Name of lesson:
Duration:
Objective: (1–2 sentence goal)
Materials needed:

◆
◆
◆
◆

Step-by-step description of the lesson:
1.
2.
3.
4.
5.

Visuals to be used:

You can see a lesson plan at the end of this unit.

9 **Developing an Assessment:** Each student for the Teach the Teacher unit not only presents in front of the class, but also assesses his or her peers for understanding. The time spent on teaching students how to create assessments is worth it. After all, designing their own tests based on their own content area allows you to see what they know as they develop questions themselves. It also teaches them the art of high-level questioning and allows students to see an assessment through a teacher's lens, thus building up their ability to take future assessments.

But you have to scaffold the process for them.

Talk about the levels of questioning. In my book, *'Tween Crayons and Curfews: Tips for Middle School Teachers*, I begin teaching levels of questioning as follows:

To begin with, I always reiterate with my students that their brain is a muscle, and like any muscle, it needs to be worked out to stay fit. School, I explain, is our gym.

"Now," I say, "If I lift a two-pound weight, will my muscle grow quickly and with tons of strength?" At this point I generally reach for a minor barbell on hand for just such an occasion.

The catcalls typically answer me with such phrases as, "No way!" and "Weak!"

"OK, but what if I work out my muscle with a twenty-five-pound weight?" I reach for a bigger barbell under my desk for this demonstration. This is generally met with the occasional, "I wanna try!" and "Let me!"

"OK," I continue. "Would you all then agree that there are activities that work your brain more rigorously then others? And would you also agree that when a brain is worked out hard, it might produce deeper knowledge then it did when it wasn't being challenged so much? And would you further agree that there are even different levels of questions, different quality of questions that, in fact, also work out your brain better than others?" I then talk to them about showing intelligent confusion . . . as a means to prove just how much we comprehend a topic.

"For that reason," I continue, "we will be looking at the different ways to ask questions, and we'll decide if they are working out our brains just a little bit or working out our brains in a way that makes them sweat."

This is when I tell them about Costa's Levels of Questioning:

Level 1: Input—I start by reciting something. If it's eighth grade, I recite "The Preamble," or if it's seventh grade, it's Shakespeare's "All the World's a Stage."

"Reciting takes a certain level of skill, don't you think?" I ask, flexing my wrists like I'm working them out with the two-pound barbell. They nod.

"But has it proven that I understand what I'm saying? Would you agree that proving that I get what's coming out of my mouth might work out my brain further?"

Level 2: Process—I then recite my respective piece again, this time with inflection and passion, punching words verbally that are important and using my face and gestures to highlight the meaning of the words.

"Now," I say. "If I were to take apart these phrases and shuffle them around, say, in sentence strips on your desk, and you were to use the words and punctuation and meaning as context clues to put them back in order, wouldn't you say that you were working out your brain more than you did before?" This time I pick up the bigger hand weights. They start to nod more, some of them moving their arms too, some showing me their biceps, knowing what's coming.

Level 3: Output—"Now let's say I were to ask you the following question . . .

'Using textual evidence, could you predict what would have been the message of the Preamble if our forefathers hadn't used the word *perfect* to describe our union? How would the ideal of our country have changed if they had used the word *acceptable*?'

or

'Do you agree with Shakespeare that people have seven ages during their lifetime? Why or why not?'

. . . would you agree that now your brain is starting to sweat just a little?" I then reach under my desk for a 100-pound barbell the class hasn't seen before. Incidentally, I'm a weakling. I can't lift it so well. Ah well, it's always good for a laugh.

Therefore, if students want to create a more challenging assessment, they won't simply focus on recall. They might want to try to ask peers to apply or hypothesize. Give them sentence stems or keywords to get their thoughts going. You can give them something like this:

Level 1—Questions that are Level 1 include sentence stems that ask them to recite, define, describe, list, etc.

Level 2—Questions that are Level 2 include sentence stems that ask them to infer, compare/contrast, sequence, categorize, etc.

Level 3—Questions that are Level 1 included sentence stems that ask them to judge, evaluate, create, hypothesize, predict, etc.

Explain that creating an assessment has to not only assess for understanding, but it must also keep students engaged. Creating a variety of questions helps to keep students on task. Here are some choices of types of questions students can develop:

- rank order questions ("please rank your knowledge of the following category from 1–5, 5 being best.");
- true/false;
- fill-in-the-blank;
- matching;
- open-ended (open-ended questions like many short answer questions ask students to apply what they know; these are more authentic but are harder to score);
- forced choice (forced choice questions actually give more power to the test maker; in other words, the students who are taking the test have no choice but to answer one way or another using only the choices provided by the test creator).

Once you've taught this concept of tiered-level questions and have taught possible question formats, have the students create a list of questions to assess their own knowledge of their topic. See Part II for an activity to help teach assessment creation, but check out the end of this chapter for an example of a student-created assessment.

Note: It might also be cool to have the students create the assessment using Google Form so that the responses automatically seed a Google Spreadsheet.

10 **Student-Created Rubric:** Have the students construct the rubrics that will go on to define their success throughout the unit. That means you'll need them to develop one for their oral presentation as well as one to score the short-answer responses for their student-created assessments. After all, even though they might be developing many multiple choice or true/false questions, they should also be encouraged to develop one or two questions that ask students to write, to justify, to explain, or to create. This takes writing informatively.

Creating a rubric can be an individual assignment or even a small group activity. The following is an excerpt from my book, '*Tween Crayons and Curfews: Tips for Middle School Teachers*.

First, you have to have the traditional rubric in front of each student. Figure 5.2 is my district rubric on writing a persuasive essay.

As you can see, it's pretty standards based and aligned to the same-old, same-old rubrics. It's got all the qualifications of what makes a great persuasive essay . . . except it's boring, and full of teacher-ese. Teacher-ese, while full of academic language, can also translate to blah-blah-blah if it's not easily understood by its intended audience: the students.

Now, starting with the numbers in the rubric, have the students (whether it's as a whole class, small group, etc.) translate what is means in their own words to get a 5, a 4, a 3, and so on.

I generally only interject my classroom monarch card once when it comes to rubric translation. I insist that the highest score should be described as "Able to Teach This Topic." Let's face it, if every opportunity to learn begins with the phrase "I don't know," then every assessment of having learned should begin with "Let me teach you what I know."

Putting the "Able to Teach This Topic" at the top of an assessment rubric serves two purposes: first, it truly assesses students in their ability to communicate, a skill that is underrated in this era of testing but which will be vital to their futures beyond school.

Figure 5.2 District Writing Rubric

PERSUASIVE COMPOSITION

Grade 7

ELA	Score 5 EXCEEDS	Score 4 MEETS	Score 3 APPROACHING	Score 2 DOES NOT MEET	Score 1 FAR BELOW
Ideas and Development	The response: • States a clear position. • Authoritatively defends position with precise/relevant evidence. • Convincingly addresses the readers' concerns.	The response: • States a general position. • Adequately defends position with relevant evidence. • Generally addresses the readers' concerns.	The response: • Weakly states a position. • Defends position with little or weak evidence. • May not address the readers' concerns.	The response: • May not state a position. • Fails to defend a position with any evidence. • Fails to address the readers' concerns.	Illegible, no response, inaccurate response, or responds in a language other than English.
Organization and Focus	• Illustrates a clear, logical organization of ideas. • Maintains a consistent focus. • Clearly addresses all parts of the writing prompt.	• Illustrates a mostly logical organization of ideas. • Maintains a mostly consistent focus. • Adequately addresses the prompt.	• Illustrates some organization of ideas. • Has an inconsistent focus. • Weakly attempts to address the prompt.	• Little or no organization is apparent. • Lacks any type of focus. • Does not address the prompt.	
Word Choice, Sentences and Paragraphs	• Exhibits use of precise, sophisticated & descriptive vocabulary. • Provides a wide and effective variety of sentence types. • Includes highly effective use of transitions. • Demonstrates effective use of multiple paragraph construction.	• Exhibits use of some precise & descriptive vocabulary. • Provides some variety of sentence types. • Includes generally effective use of transitions. • Demonstrates adequate use of multiple paragraph construction.	• Exhibits use of mostly simplistic (basic and elementary) vocabulary. • Provides a limited variety of sentence types. • May include ineffective or awkward transitions. • Demonstrates weak use of multiple paragraph construction.	• Exhibits consistent use of simplistic (basic & elementary) vocabulary, and/or needless repetition. • Uses mostly short, simple sentences, and/or makes frequent errors in sentence construction. • Does not use transitions. • Demonstrates little of no use of multiple paragraph construction.	
Grammar, Usage, Mechanics and Spelling	• Contains few, if any, errors in the conventions of the English language. • Errors do not impede the understanding of the writing.	• Contains some errors in conventions of the English language. • Errors do not impede the understanding of the writing.	• Contains numerous errors in the conventions of the English language. • Errors impede the understanding of the writing.	• Contains many serious errors in the conventions of the English language. • Errors seriously impede the understanding of the writing.	

Second, it brings a respect for teaching into the classroom, and that's not a bad thing. "Able to Teach" should be the acme of A grades, and by defining the highest grade in a phrase form rather than a letter, students can better understand their goal.

Go through each row of expectations, creating a gradation of accomplishment in their own words. Figure 5.3 shows how my seventh grade fared in its own rubric translation.

Additionally, see Figure 5.4 for an example of an oral presentation rubric created by my eighth grade class for our Teach the Teacher unit. The whole class can design the rubric or each individual student can develop his or her own rubric upon which he or she wishes to be assessed.

It's all about goal setting, being upfront with the students, and giving them ownership of their own learning by teaching them the secrets of teaching as a craft.

11 **Oral Presentation Timing Sheet:** Before students get up in front of a classroom to present their lessons, they need to practice, practice, practice. One scaffolded way to help them practice is to have them fill out a timing sheet. The timing sheet helps them assess their own speed and pacing as they speak out loud. Some kids really need to see the numbers in order to believe they are speeding. That's because the voice in our heads sounds perfectly fine, whereas from an audience's point of view, our voices come out differently. (See a blank timing sheet template in Part II.)

12 **Visual for Oral Presentation:** Guide kids to create high-quality visuals to highlight their oral presentations. Remind them that no great teacher would only speak to an audience as a means to convey a lesson. It's about making sure that multiple modalities are tapped and topics are illustrated visually as well as audibly.

There are some basic rules I've put together in a handout for students that can be found in Part II. They are meant to help give them some limitations and guidelines for creating PowerPoints, Keynotes, Google Presentations, and Prezis.

13 **Oral Presentation:** As they determined when they developed their rubrics, being Able to Teach is the highest form of proving comprehension. This unit culminates in students role-playing as teachers and instructing a classroom of peers in how to develop a particular skill.

The elements of the presentation must include the following elements:

◆ It must be a combination of different examples of multiple intelligences.
◆ It must include a visual of some kind (PowerPoint, poster, video, etc.).
◆ It must include an activity for the students in the classroom (or representatives pulled from the captive audience of peers). For instance, perhaps the class lines up at a free throw line, and after observing the student model how to throw a great free throw, they are given the opportunity, one by one, to try their hand at the task.

14 **Backchanneling Questions:** Meanwhile, the audience of students aren't sitting back and relaxing during the presentations. Nope. While students are presenting, the audience will be on Google, typing questions onto a document as they think them. It's all about assessing one's ability to question, and it's a digital version of Think Aloud.

Figure 5.3 Student-Created Rubric

ELA	5 – Able to Teach	4 – It Gets There	3 – Not Quite, Try Harder	2 – Are You Listening?	1 – Epic Fail
Ideas (what thoughts went into it?)	• Great thesis statement that's a map of the essay • Great evidence, quotes • Great counterargument that says "OK, I get that there are others whom don't agree with me and WHY"	• Good thesis that says what you're going to prove • Good evidence (quotes, personal experience) • Says there are those who don't agree, but don't give them a lot of time to explain why they understand why	• Thesis is there somewhere in intro • Only some evidence, but not for each point • Only says in one line that there are those who disagree (that's not fair)	• What's this paper about? • No evidence (you didn't prove it!) • Not one mention of people who disagree	Can't read it, not a persuasive essay
Organization and Focus (can your reader follow it?)	• Really clear, like building blocks from one idea to another • Bull's-eye every time! • Every piece of the prompt is included clearly	• The reader can definitely follow the logic • Generally stays on target • I can find all prompt somewhere	• Um, I think I get where you're going with this • Drifts! • Tries to answer the prompt, but is missing something	• I don't follow you • Blurry, like dirt on your glasses, unfocused • Doesn't answer the prompt	
Word Choice, Paragraphs, Sentences	• Really high-level words! • Tons of sentence types and lengths (texture) • Great transitions (to quote, to commentary, between paragraphs) • Good use of paragraphs to divide ideas	• Good, grade level vocab • Some sentence variety • A few transition words or phrases here and there • Uses multiple paragraphs	• Simple vocab (good, happy, nice, fine, etc...) • Only one kind of sentence/gets boring in the rhythm • Bumpy transitions! • Doesn't seem to understand why you need paragraphs	• Repeats key words over and over • Simple sentences • No transitions (reader must jump across gaps!) • One LOOONNGG paragraph	
Conventions (do your errors get in the way for your reader?)	• Only a couple of errors (like a really good rough draft)	• Some errors, but they don't get in the way	• Lots of errors but the readers still understand what the author means	• What the heck did the author mean by that?!	

Figure 5.4 Oral Presentation Rubric

Trait	100–90%	89–80%	79–70%	69–60%	What did you think would happen?
Persuasive *pitching yourself *conviction *holds one's interest					
Visual/Model					
Presentation *appearance *posture *nerves (dancing) *eye contact *inflection					
Content *research *length *word choice *applicable					

The students have already been introduced to Costa's Levels of Questioning because they've already developed the assessments they will distribute when it's their turn to present. But as the audience, they are going to once again trigger the use of those concepts to prove they are interacting with the presenter.

To do this, you can share a document with the class using Google Drive as a means for students to type in their questions publicly, real time, as their fellow students present. An offline version might look like a large poster on each small group's table that would allow students to write questions as they think them.

To backchannel, however, takes using a tech device of some kind, be it iPad, Chromebook, or smartphone. A backchannel, for those who don't know the word, is like the B-story conversation that might be going on beneath the main A-story of the presentation. The students on the backchannel are having a conversation or asking questions of the presenter while it is happening in real time.

Twitter is a form of a backchannel. It asks participants to construct their responses or shares in 140 characters or fewer. This limitation demands the participant to get to the point quickly, and it's a powerful limitation in the classroom as well.

When I backchannel with my students during presentation, I prep a Google Document (see Figure 5.5) ahead of time for each period with the list of presenters already entered in the order in which they were to present. I used subheadings to divide them into dates.

Another tool you could use is todaysmeet.com. Todaysmeet is also a great, classroom-friendly backchannel program that allows you to close the room after a certain amount of time. However, to have a successful backchannel conversation going on simultaneously to other speakers presenting takes setting up norms early on. You can see the norms for backchanneling that I use in my classroom in Part II of this book.

Anyway, as students presented, I could watch as the audience's questions lit up the Google Doc. You could tell what presentations resonated or made the students really think because the high-level questions were quicker to come. And generally, as really great questions appeared, they would inspire students to revise their lower-level questions

Figure 5.5 Google Doc of Presenters

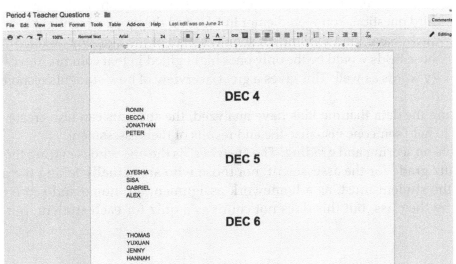

or devise follow-ups to those already asked. In other words, the kids were learning from each other. The transparency of the document engaged everyone and encouraged the best from them all.

In the end, many students who were normally quiet were encouraged by the ability to type their voice in class, and I had a chance to see them all think aloud through their real-time writing. Students were loosely scored on quantity of questions and the number of higher-level (Level 2 or 3) questions.

Once the presentation was completed, students could ask their questions verbally. It was great when the presenter answered these questions eloquently on the fly, but to be honest, that wasn't what I was assessing. Instead, I was assessing those who asked the questions.

15 Administering, Scoring, and Analyzing Scored Quiz Responses: At the end of the lesson, the "teacher" will administer the quiz he or she constructed. If it is created using Google Forms, the responses will automatically seed into a spreadsheet. Otherwise, students should record responses using something like Excel. The spreadsheet of results gives students tons of data from which to pull in order to cite evidence for their business letter to their administrator.

Have the students score the assessments by hand for the utmost impact. Sure, they can use something like Flubaroo or other add-ons out there, but it's powerful for them to score them by hand too. Also have the students use the student-created writing rubrics to score their short-answer responses.

Looking at the spreadsheet can give them all kinds of insight into what students know and don't know as well as what their peers like and dislike.

One easy way to view specific answers in a Google Spreadsheet is to use the Conditional Formatting tool under the Format tab on the Menu bar. Here's how to do it:

1. Highlight the column whose responses you want to check.
2. From there, click on Format.
3. Drop down to Conditional Formatting.
4. Enter in the text about which you want information, and pick a highlighting color. For instance, let's say you want to see how many students marked "A" on the third question. You would enter in "A" and then pick a highlight color.
5. Click "Save" and the student should see all of the kids who entered "A" because those fields would be the only ones highlighted in that column. You can also specify words as well. This gives a great overview of how students responded.

Using the data that the kids have analyzed, the students can also create graphs and charts to help someone visualize the end results of their assessment.

Note on scoring and grading: The "teacher" is the one who is getting the equivalent of a quiz grade for the assessment, not those who are actually taking the assessment. True, the student must, as a homework assignment, go home and score the quizzes taken by the class, but this does not count as a quiz for each student, but rather as a participation or class work grade. After all, it is more meant to assess the student as a teacher and to keep the class accountable for behavior and focus during the lesson's presentation.

16 **Persuasive Letter to Administrator:** This final component of the Teach the Teacher unit is an authentic assessment wherein the student writes a letter to an administrator to convince him or her that the chosen activity or hobby or whatever should either be an elective at the school or should be highlighted as the most important lesson of the year. So, in other words, you might have letters proving:

> Skateboarding Should Be Its Own Elective, or
> The Pythagorean Theorem Is the Most Applicable Lesson Learned This Year

To see an outline of a formal business letter, go to Part II in this book. See a student example at the end of this chapter.

In the past, I've gotten different school stakeholders to agree to help in the scoring process as an authentic audience for this final written assessment. The principal, assistant principals, even a couple Board of Ed members have all chipped in to score a few letters each and to give written feedback based on the student-developed argument-writing rubric. They were instructed to pretend it was a real pitch for the elective and to respond with great seriousness. In a past book I expand on this unit as follows:

> Sure, it was a mythical program, but many of the administrators actually got really into it, highlighting their feedback on the rubric prior to issuing a score and even writing comments as to why or why not they would consider the addition of such an elective. Here is a comment written by our principal in response to one such persuasive letter:
>
> > *No, sorry Brian. We won't be offering naptime as an elective for next year. I do, however appreciate your research on the sleep needs of the average middle schooler, and I was also very interested in your studies of dream symbolism. Nevertheless, naptime, however necessary, is, unfortunately, not covered in the state standards, and will not be on the master calendar for next year.*

Having the students write to other members of the educational community creates not only authenticity, but also a community that extends beyond your classroom. It also lets folks know of the great stuff going on in your own classroom.

In the end, the Teach the Teacher unit is meant to assess students not only on content but also on communication, and it's this very act of being able to communicate content that we should all be striving to assess. After all, when these students leave our year behind, eventually leaving school behind entirely, they must take with them the ability to share, to create, to assess, to problem solve, to research . . . to teach.

Yours is the profession that teaches all others. Prepare them with this in mind, and you will have had a hand in whatever their future holds.

Tip on How to Assess Writing Quickly #5

Train students to give feedback to each other first. In the spirit of training students to be teachers, put them in the role of "first feedback-er" by pairing them up to give advice to each other before you ever see their final draft. As I say in *'Tween Crayons and Curfews: Tips for Middle School Teachers*:

> Train the students to be able to give a first wave of feedback in earlier stages of their learning. This not only saves you from having to wade through writing the same basic comments over and over that could have been easily caught by a peer, but it also trains them to know what you need to see, thus eliminating some of the errors in the first place.

Teach students to be teachers and you will share the load of assessing their writing so you can move them forward with their content.

Student Exemplars

Problem Statement

Obesity has been an issue in the United States for many years. Capable of causing many health issues, obesity affects both adults and children. Obesity can cause many diseases, affecting 34.9% (about seven out of twenty) of adults and 16.9% (approximately one out of five) of children, according to Food Research and Action Center. It can cause Diabetes, High Blood Pressure, Coronary Artery Disease, Coronary Vascular Disease, Heart Attack, stroke, and even cancer, as reported by Arizona State University. Obesity causes excessive cholesterol to build up in one's arteries, therefore clogging blood vessels, and causing strokes or heart attacks. Also, obesity could cause Diabetes. The most common type of diabetes, known as type 2 diabetes, which affects, according to Arizona State University, about ninety to 95 percent of Hispanic Americans, has to do with how there isn't enough insulin (the substance in the human body which neutralizes sugar) to eliminate threatening sugar in the body. This process may lead to coma, or in severe cases, death. To solve this predicament, I propose teach a lesson in how obesity could be prevented, because making students aware of obesity and its capabilities is crucial to ending its reign on our future.

Questions:

1. Why do people become obese?
2. Why do people go from using food as fuel to using it for other purposes?
3. How do people lose weight in a healthy way?
4. How does the weight of our people affect money spent on health?

Lesson Plan—Spreading Germs

Lesson name: Spreading germs

Duration: Whole class period

Objective: The objective for this experiment is to see if protecting yourself from germs actually makes a difference from not protecting yourself.

Materials needed:

- Students
- Post-it notes
- A classroom

Step-by-step description of the lesson:

1. 5 minute lecture on how germs spread

    Visual used: Video on protecting yourself from germs (cartoon for kids) http://youtu.be/O5PwLAZNnKc

2. Activity/Demo:
    - Everyone will be handed a bunch of post-it notes.
    - Divide the classroom into two groups of people.
    - One half won't be trying to protect or contain the germs.
    - The other half of the class will try to protect and contain the germs.
    - Then the students will just go on with the class period as usual.
    - Whenever a student comes in contact with anything (i.e. a classmate/friend, table, etc.) put a post-it note on it.
    - At the end of the class period, the post-it notes on each side will be counted up.
    - We will see if protecting and containing the disease makes a difference from not protecting and containing the disease.

3. Assessment

Works Cited

"This Is How Germs Spread … It's Sickening!" *This Is How Germs Spread … It's Sickening!* N.p., n.d. Web. 06 Dec. 2014. <www.health.ny.gov/publications/7110/>.

"Infectious Diseases." *Germs: Understand and Protect against Bacteria, Viruses and Infection.* Mayo Clinic Staff, n.d. Web. 06 Dec. 2014. <www.mayoclinic.org/diseases-conditions/infectious-diseases/in-depth/germs/art-20045289>.

"What Are Germs?" *KidsHealth—the Web's Most Visited Site about Children's Health.* Ed. Steven Dowshen. The Nemours Foundation, 01 Jan. 2014. Web. 05 Dec. 2014. <http://kidshealth.org/kid/talk/qa/germs.html>.

Name:_____   **Date:_____**

Metals - An Introduction to My Metals and Minerals Collection

1. **Compare and contrast** thermal conductivity and electrical conductivity using the graphic organizer.

2. **Recall.** Fill in the Blank: Metals are _____ that are good _____ of electric current and _____.

3. **Theorize.** Why do metals tend to decrease as you move from left to right across the periodic table?
   _____
   _____
   _____

4. **Explain** the reason of corrosion.
   _____
   _____

5. **Recall**. What is the meaning of the word "ductile?"
A. flexible
B. brittle
C. unyielding
D. intractable

6. **Match** the word and the definition (definitions were found using Quizlet.com)

Metals	the ability of an object to transfer heat
Reactivity	the gradual wearing away of a metal due to a chemical reaction
Corrosion	the ease and speed with which a substance reacts with other substances
Thermal Conductivity	elements that are good conductors of electric current and heat

7. **Recall.** True or False?
   Alkaline earth metals are from Group 1 of the Periodic Table.

   _____

8. **List.** What are at least 10 metals in the Periodic Table of Elements?

9. **Hypothesize.** What gets fireworks off the ground?
   _____
   _____
   _____

10. **Create** a question about copper.
    _____
    _____

Works Cited

"Quizlet." *Quizlet*. Web. 30 Dec. 2014. <http://quizlet.com/>.

Business Letter

Edward T.
Jefferson Middle School
1372 E. las Tunas Dr.
San Gabriel, CA 91776

Dec. 14, 2014

Dr. Yuen
District Office
408 Junipero Serra Drive
San Gabriel, CA 91776

Dear Dr. Yuen:

Butterflies in your stomach. Heart racing. Nausea. These are the feelings that many people get when called up to present a speech. Whether it's in front of a small group of people or one hundred people, public speaking is one of the greatest phobias in our country today. However, speaking in front of a big audience is an essential skill in life. According to Boundless, 75% of people have a fear of public speaking, and only through daily practice will we fight this fear. For this reason, I firmly believe that Mock Trial should be made an elective.

People have fear as a result of lack of confidence, and mock trial will help eliminate it. In general, as you get up on stage, the hypothalamus, generates the pituitary gland to secrete the hormone ACTH, which then stimulates the Adrenal Glands in your kidneys. As a result, it releases adrenaline through your blood, causing you to be scared. That's why schools are offering classes to help build this trait in students.

Mock Trial is a challenging role-playing competition, where students compete in their county. The competition is an imitation criminal trial, where students are cast as attorneys, witnesses and court officers. They argue a case in front of a real judge and practicing attorneys, who then evaluate how well you did. By participating in this elective, students will, therefore, learn more about our criminal justice law system (and how not to get caught up in it!), build up their self-confidence, develop their analytical abilities, and enhance their ability to collaborate with others, not to mention the real goal: building up their public speaking skills.

Mock Trial also builds up your writing skills through writing direct and cross-examinations. Being part of Mock Trial becomes necessary to think deeply about the case in order to draw clear conclusions. It takes critical thinking to look through a witness's statement, finding facts where you can use it against the witness, which increases note taking skills.

For these reasons Mock Trial really should be offered as an elective for it helps you develop important skills, and prepares you for when it's your time to make your mark.

Thank you for considering my argument, and please feel free to contact me with any further questions about my research for this activity.

Sincerely,

Edward T.

Part II

Mix-and-Match Lessons to Design Your Own PBL Units

Google Advanced Search

Today, we will be looking at Google Advanced Search and doing an activity regarding developing questions as search functions.

- Go to www.google.com.

- Let's say you are researching for an argument essay on games used in education. Type in *video games in school.*

- How many hits do you get? _____

Geesh! That's a lot. Google is asking you to go through how many pages? And I bet not all of them even apply to the topic you are looking for.

Some say Google makes you dumber; but I say that we have to be smarter to make Google do the work for us.

- Now go to www.google.com/advanced_search.

- You'll see all kinds of fields you can customize to make Google do the work for you.

- In the first field, type in a specific question, the most specific you can think of, that is related to the topic.

- In the Language field, select English.

- In the Region field, select United States.

- In the Last Update field, select past month.

- In the usage rights field, select free to use or share.

- Now click Advanced Search.

- If you look at the Google menu, you will see a button called Search Tools. Click that.

- Now, how many hits do you have? _____

Six Steps of Being an Internet Detective

Researching Reliably

Being An Internet Detective: The Six Accuracy Steps Handout

The best part of the Internet is also the most suspicious part: the fact that anyone can write anything. The Internet is exciting because you have access to experts and information that your parents and grandparents never had access to. You can take a college level class, you can study any subject you want, and you can find the answers to almost anything. But it also means that anyone can put up a website that is false or misleading, and you don't want to fall for it.

Computers may be fast, but they aren't smart. That's where you come in. You need to check websites for accuracy before you use their information as fact. Here are six steps to check for accuracy:

☐ **Use Your Common Sense**

Ask questions. Asking questions is a sure sign of how smart you are. As you read website content, make sure you always ask yourself the following questions:

- Who is the author of this site?
- Is there evidence to support what the author is saying?
- Is there evidence somewhere that supports or disagrees with this author?
- Is this author biased?

☐ **Verify the Evidence**

Be a detective with everything you read. The answers all lie in the evidence. Keep on the lookout for:

- proper nouns
- dates
- important keywords

Take this embedded information to a search engine (like Google) and find other believable references to back up your information.

☐ **Triangulate the Data**

Look at the word "triangulate." The prefix is "tri-," which means _____. What this means is that if you can't find three sources to back up your fact, then you can't really know for sure if your fact is credible or not. Read suspiciously!

©Teacher Created Resources, Inc.

Researching Reliably

Being An Internet Detective:
The Six Accuracy Steps Handout *(cont.)*

☐ **Follow the Links**

To where a page links is as important as what information is on that actual page. Click on the external links to find the next layer of information about the author and his or her intent. Perhaps you'll be linked to an encyclopedia entry (reliable link), or perhaps you'll be directed to an Amazon or Café Press product (unreliable link). Don't fall for a website that's really an elaborate ad to sell someone's product or point of view!

☐ **Analyze The URL**

This is by no means foolproof, but it is a place to start in verifying the accuracy of the site.

☐ **Check the Publisher**

If possible, use websites like **easywhois.com** to check the background on the site to help you answer some of the questions in your head.

By checking off your accuracy checklist, you will have diminished the chances that you have fallen for a false website or a website that is more promotional than fact.

Congratulations! You are now an Internet Detective.

How to Write a Newspaper Article

Some of how we learn to write is by recognizing the components that make up a good document. Print out an article from a website such as www.cnn.com/studentnews or https://newsela.com/. It can be on a topic of your own choice.

Annotate your article as follows:

◆ Circle the Who.

◆ Put a square around the What.

◆ Make a squiggly line under the When.

◆ Make a cloud around the Where.

◆ Put brackets around the sentences that explain Why or How.

As you write your own newspaper article, remember the following:

◆ No bias: stick to the facts.

◆ Pick a stance and be consistent: figure out the point of view and don't deviate from it.

◆ KISS: keep it simple, silly! Many fun narrative elements such as figurative language are used sparingly in newspaper articles.

The newspaper article that you will be writing must have the following elements:

1. a headline

2. a byline

3. an embedded image with a caption

4. the article itself.

The Problem Statement

You are going to be developing what is called a "problem statement." In terms of college and career readiness, a problem statement is used anywhere from a doctorate thesis to a business proposal. It states the goal for your research and the problem you wish to solve. Ultimately, it is meant to help the focus the topic of your persuasive TED speech.

To create a problem statement, you must write a paragraph that includes the following information:

1. States the broad problem/topic that you are interested in researching.
2. Defines the problem you will be solving by narrowing the issue.
3. Describes why it needs to be investigated by giving background information and context.
4. States your goals in writing and researching this problem (I will . . ., I plan . . ., I would like . . ., I propose . . ., etc.).

From there, you will develop three to five questions based on the problem statement. These specific questions will further serve to guide your writing. By answering them through your investigation, you should then more easily find a solution or answer to your problem, which will be a main focus of your persuasive speech.

Here is an example of a completed problem statement and five corresponding questions that are specific to our speech-writing assignment. Notice how the paragraph starts out broad in its scope and narrows down to a more specific goal:

Bullying has long been a problem with children and adults alike. While bullying can be seen even in the workplace among adults, those who bully as grown-ups may also be those who bully as children. Children all over our country are victims of bullying, but bullying comes in many forms, some physical and some mental. We must combat this plague from many different angles in order to make bullies uncomfortable in their intimidation. I propose to write an argumentation speech that investigates the different forms of bullying and how we can band together to stop it.

Questions:

1. What are the forms of bullying?
2. What defines bullying?
3. Can a bully be reformed?
4. What are methods a victim can use to stop being bullied?
5. What can schools, the government, laws, families do to invest in solving this problem?

Writing with Numeracy Lesson

Textual *evidence* can be found in the form of both words and numbers. Sure, we use anecdotal evidence and personal experience as a form of evidence, but those aren't the most convincing because they show *bias*. However, a more solid form of evidence can be found in numerical data. Throughout this unit, you will be expected to provide proof of your findings in evidence presented in writing, in *infographics*, and in numbers. *Graphs*, *stats*, and *polls* will also play a part in your final submission. All of these methods and more will help convince an audience of the importance of your issue.

When writing with numbers, there are a few rules of thumb. Please note that not every rule here is universally accepted. These are the general rules for many experts:

1. Numbers that start a sentence are in words.
   Ten years ago, the factory was a vibrant community of employees.

   Your example:

2. Spell out double-digit whole numbers that are single words. Use numerals for numbers made up of two words.
   Eventually, twenty students came forward with bullying accusations.
   Eventually, the entire team of 24 came forward with bullying accusations.

   Your example:

3. Always spell out simple fractions and use hyphens with them.
   According to the World Health Organization, one-half of the children in the country have been affected by this disease.

   Your example:

4. Round numbers are usually spelled out.
   People use around fifteen hundred plastic bottles a second, according to Watershed.com.

   Your example:

5. Use numbers when expressing decimals.
   According to the Federal Food and Drug Administration, it would only cost $0.10 per family to provide them with this resource.

   Your example:

6. Decades should be spelled out in words.
   The Seventies marked an entirely different decade than the one that preceded it.

   Your example:

7. Spell out ordinal numbers.
   The first time he spoke in front of an audience, he felt weak in the knees.

   Your example:

8. Use numbers for times (if using a.m. or p.m.) and for dates (years and days).
   The earthquake struck at 7 a.m. on March 21, 2010.

   Your example:

9. Do not use "from" or "between" before a hyphenated date range. It's meaningless.
   Use: From 1986 to 1987, the city was struggling to maintain its level of economic growth.
   Don't Use: From 1986–1987, the city was struggling to maintain its level of economic growth.

   Your example:

10. Generally, 0–9 are spelled out. Numbers after 9 are written in numerical form (unless they are single-word numbers, i.e., twenty, thirty; see rule #2).
All three students used their cell phones to access their assignment.
All 11 students used their cell phones to text their responses to their teachers.

Your example:

Other resources in writing with numbers:

Celia M. Elliot, University of Illinois, Writing Numbers in Technical Documents: http://people.physics.illinois.edu/Celia/Lectures/Numbers.pdf
Business Writing Blog, Rules on Writing Numbers: www.businesswritingblog.com/business_writing/2006/03/rules_on_writin.html

Researchable websites for data and statistics that may help your advocacy speech:

World Health Organization: www.who.int/en/
Journalist's Toolbox, Writing with Numbers: www.spjvideo.org/jtb/archive/writing-with-numbers/
Gapminder (fact-based world view): www.gapminder.org/

Found more? Send them to your teacher to add to this growing list of resources!

Collaboration Constitution Assignment

You need to design a contract that all group members will sign. Look at the following websites as you begin to develop your charter. You can use some of the format and language to help you develop your document:

- *Life Cycle Engineering*, Team Charters: What Are They and What's Their Purpose?: www.lce.com/Team_Charters_What_are_they_and_whats_their_purpose_360-item.html
- *MindTools*, Team Charters: www.mindtools.com/pages/article/newTMM_95.htm
- *Team Helper*, Sample Team Charter: www.teamhelper.com/sample/TC_GuideSample.pdf

Think about the following as you draft your team charter. You are not limited to these questions and your final document should use multiple text structures to communicate your contract.

1. What will be the roles and/or responsibilities of each member of the team as they relate to the project?
2. How often will you meet outside of school?
3. How will you communicate outside of school (using email, Skype, virtual classroom, phone, etc.)?
4. How much time passes before a reply to a question or comment is considered unacceptable?
5. What script can you develop or sentence stem can you use to tell others they aren't holding their weight or participating the way they should?
6. What strategies can you develop in order to increase participation from members before coming to the teacher for intervention?
7. What are your deadlines?
8. What are the roles/responsibilities of each member as it relates to running the group? In other words, is there a group leader, recorder, timer, etc.?
9. What are the norms of your meetings?
10. Begin your collaboration constitution with a mission statement. A mission statement is an agreed upon set of goals that you all are setting out to accomplish. For instance:

    The mission of our group, the _____ League, is to collaborate in order to develop the highest _____ we can present. We will use our individual talents to help other, and we will abide by the rules of our constitution in order to accomplish your goals.

11. You will end your group charter with lines to be signed by all members of your team.

How to Comment on a Blog

Netiquette: How to Comment on a Blog

Online reading is meant to be very interactive. While there are those students who click around reading this and that, there are many who also comment on what they read. In fact, commenting is not only accepted, it's encouraged. Remember that just as there are classroom rules for responding to someone's writing and ideas, there are rules online when you are responding to a blog post or article. Here are some of the rules:

1. **Don't say anything you wouldn't say in person.** Just because you can't see the author doesn't mean he or she doesn't have feelings.

2. **Don't hijack the discussion.** Stay on topic.

3. **Bring something new to the conversation.**

4. **Don't be a know-it-all smarty-pants.** If you have to correct somebody, be polite. And you don't always need to be the one to correct somebody. Think of it like class: if all the students corrected each other every time someone misspoke or mispronounced, nobody would feel comfortable speaking out loud. It's the same online. It's more important to focus on the deeper content when reading.

5. **Make your tone clear.** Try not to use humor or sarcasm; they don't always go over well, even if you are the best writer ever. Use emoticons or write what the audience might see at that moment (shrug) to communicate your message clearer.

6. **Don't write anonymously.**

7. **Cite your sources with links.** If you mention a resource, link the words to the resource or provide the website for others to refer to.

8. **Paste quotes into your comment field.** If you are commenting on a quote within the post, copy and paste the quote into your comment field and then comment on it below so that the readers don't have to scroll back up to the original article.

9. **Don't comment when you are emotional.** If you are angry with someone for posting something, calm down before writing something that could forever be accessed. A good rule is to give it a day and then return to the post. Maybe even write a draft of your comment and let it lie for 24 hours. You can always cut and paste it into the comment field if you still believe it represents you well.

10. **Don't fan a flash fire.** A flash fire is when someone says something inflammatory and then people jump on the bandwagon, fanning the flames even more. If you ever see it happening, don't jump in. If there is a moderator, let him or her know what's happening. That will defuse it even faster.

Online Ethics and Copyright Activity

As we continue working online, it's important that we become more mindful of using online resources ethically. Read the required pieces and answer the corresponding questions. Please note that from here on in, I will expect that all photos and music used in your digital projects be cited properly. This citation can either be compiled at the end of a project, on a page devoted to this purpose, or cited under each and every image as "courtesy of . . ." Got it?

1. Go to Google and type in "define: ethics." Based on the results, in your own words, what is the definition of "ethics"?

2. Go to the Learn the Web website at www.learnthenet.com/index.php/flashtest/ netiquette.htm. In the left-hand menu, you'll see "Test Yourself." Take the test. How did you score on your "netiquette savvy"?

3. Go to the About page on Creative Commons at www.creativecommons.org. In your own words, what is the purpose of this website?

4. Go to Google Advanced Search. Find the drop-down tab that allows you to find free fair-use sites from which to pull images or documents. Using Google Advanced Search, find one free, fair-use, image-based website to suggest to another student. What is the URL of this website?

5. Watch the video on the four factors of fair use from the MIT library. You can find it at http://techtv.mit.edu/videos/4882. What are the four factors we consider when we evaluate for fair use? Please use bullet points to identify these four points.

6. Go to the About page on the Library of Congress copyright website at http:// copyright.gov/about/. Read the page, and summarize the gist of that page in a paragraph (200 words or less).

7. The final piece is a contract of sorts. Type your name below as a signature of understanding of the following statement: *I understand that every image and piece of music must be cited on every project from here on in throughout this school year.*

Understanding Infographics Lesson

1. What is an infographic?
    Look at the following infographic and answer the questions below:
    www.customermagnetism.com/infographics/what-is-an-infographic/

    ◆   An infographic is "a data-rich _____ of a thesis."

    ◆   What percent of information transmitted to the brain is visual? _____
        percent.

    ◆   What percent of people respond better to visual information than to text? _____
        percent.

2. Analyzing an infographic
    Once done, look at the following infographic from Princeton University and answer
    the following question:
    www.princeton.edu/ina/infographics/water.html

    Examine it closely, and then analyze the infographic in one to four paragraphs.
    Remember to cite the graphic specifically as evidence for your analysis. Each of the
    following questions does not need to be in its own paragraph. Instead, find a way to
    organize your thoughts so that your short-answer essay includes all of the necessary
    responses.

    ◆   Based on what you know about the components of the word, what does the word
        "infographic" mean?

    ◆   What is the overarching issue that the infographic describes?

    ◆   An infographic is like an essay, but it uses symbols, images, text, and data
        to prove and persuade. It is rich with information. What was the most stunning
        or interesting piece of information that you learned from this graphic?

    ◆   What symbols were used to create this infographic? Feel free to bullet your
        responses.

    ◆   Looking at text structure, how does the artist highlight a particular topic or draw
        your attention to a particular element?

    ◆   Who are the sources of this information?

Executive Summary Outline

Imagine you are a busy executive. You don't have time to read a 10-page report on a theory about how to solve a problem. What you need is an executive summary. The purpose of an executive summary is to inform a reader quickly about a complex topic, so the document must be simple and easy to read so that anyone can understand the issue and the proposed solution. An executive summary does the following:

- summarizes the main points of your issue
- analyzes the most important points
- recommends a solution.

A rough outline could be (think of these as sections, not necessarily as paragraphs):

a. Background information
   i. What is the purpose of the report?
   ii. What is the scope of the issue?

b. Main points
   i. Major findings/arguments
   ii. Concrete evidence
      1. Data
      2. Videos
      3. Infographics
      4. Interviews, polls, surveys
   iii. Methods currently used to solve the problem
   iv. How to publicize the issue

c. Final recommendations

Note:

- Keep language strong and positive
- No more than 2–3 pages in length
- Consider using subtitles, bold, or bullets to help organize your document
- Short, readable paragraphs

Remember to keep the six traits in mind. You can never write without them close at hand: sentence variety, voice, word choice, proper conventions, great ideas, easy to follow organization.

Oral Presentation Timing Sheet

There's all kinds of things to think about when presenting an oral presentation: volume, pronunciation, posture, etc. But one of the things that really trips up students is pacing. That is, they have a tendency to speed when they get nervous.

Great speakers practice to get as good as they can be before speaking in front of others. Everyone, after all, gets nervous.

The general rule of thumb is that three-quarters of a page is about a minute of speech. So, when you're writing and practicing, you should know how to pace yourself and keep yourself from speeding as you present.

The following is an activity that will help you to time out your presentation beat by beat.

1. First time through: Say your speech the whole way through without stopping. Mark your time here: _____

2. Second time through: Do it in slow motion. Say your speech super slow one full time. Try to double your original time. Try to get your four-minute speech to take eight minutes. It'll feel weird, but try to stay in control of your speed so your nerves don't take control of you. Mark your time here: _____

3. Third time through: After you do a slo-mo speech, try to go back to a more normal pacing. After doing it slowly, however, you should be slowing down with each practice. Mark your time here: _____

4. For every time you practice, mark your time here: _____ _____ _____

5. Reflect: What were you feeling that made you speed?

What strategies did you use/can you use to help you slow down?

Norms for Backchanneling and Using Twitter

1. Always have the backchannel open in a public place (LCD projector, public monitor, etc.).

2. Have students use their initials or username to identify who said what. For instance:

   ◆ HW: When preparing for a test, make sure the lesson is the last thing you read before bed. (89 characters)

3. Make sure to set expectations for topics of what students can backchannel about. Some basic ways to participate are as follows:

   ◆ questioning something that was said/read;
   ◆ relating to something that was said/read;
   ◆ comparing a topic with a metaphor or simile;
   ◆ predicting where something is heading;
   ◆ visualizing a topic;
   ◆ evaluating/giving your academic opinion on a topic;
   ◆ answering a prompt or question that was posed;
   ◆ taking Cornell Notes.

4. Have students practice backchanneling offline first. In other words, have students respond to prompts in 140 characters or fewer on a piece of paper or post-it. For instance, you can:

   ◆ Give them a subject-specific paragraph and have them squeeze a summary down to 140 characters on a piece of paper.
   ◆ Ask them a content-related question to respond to as an exit card.
   ◆ Have students develop 140 character questions to ask each other.

5. When students are *not* typing in the backchannel conversation, their monitors should be at a 45-degree angle to show they are paying attention.

Internet Literacy: Verifying the Evidence Lesson

Today, we are going to be practicing our research skills. We will be researching the validity of an excerpt from Wikipedia, the scourge of all academic research!

Here is a reminder of where you can find out information about MLA formatting: https://owl.english.purdue.edu/owl/resource/747/08/

Here is where you can have EasyBib help you cite your findings properly: www.easybib.com/reference/guide/mla/website

Go to the Wikipedia article on Henry Wadsworth Longfellow and read it: http://en.wikipedia.org/wiki/Henry_Wadsworth_Longfellow

1. In the following space, list 10 keywords or data that are hyperlinked in the passage.

_____   _____

_____   _____

_____   _____

_____   _____

_____   _____

2. Select three of the keywords you have listed, and convert each one into a question to type into Google. For instance, you might type the following into Google:

Did Longfellow write "Paul Revere's Ride"?

3. Using MLA format, cite three websites that confirm the information you learned on Wikipedia. Remember, you can have EasyBib do all the formatting work for you! (See prior link.)

Question #1:

Citation:

Citation:

Citation:

Question #2:

Citation:

Citation:

Citation:

Question #3:

Citation:

Citation:

Citation:

Cornell Notes

Name:

Course name:

Period:

Date:

Title is a driving, overall question

List of questions	Notes

Summary

Oral Presentation Rubric

Volume – Can I hear you from the back of the room?	1	2	3	4	5
Emphasis – Does your voice sound textured and interesting or is it monotone and flat? How much passion is in your tone?	1	2	3	4	5
Stance/Poise – Are you rocking and rolling? Are you leaning on anything? Are you fidgeting or are your hands in your pockets?	1	2	3	4	5
Cohesiveness/Overall Presentation – Have you clearly practiced with your visuals and text? Are you "dressed for success" ready to present for an audience? Are you pronouncing all words correctly? Have you put thought into where to stand and where your visuals are?	1	2	3	4	5
Eye Contact – Are you memorized enough that you aren't trapped to your index cards or to the screen behind you? Are you making connections with your audience?	1	2	3	4	5
Other _____	1	2	3	4	5

Business Letter Outline

Your street
City, State, Zip

Date

Contact's name
Title
Organization name
Street address
City, state, zip

Dear Mr. or Ms. (person's last name only)

Paragraph 1: State immediately the position you are pursuing and how you came to know of the opening. Explain your interest in applying.

Paragraph 2: Share your talents, education, and past experience that make you a perfect candidate. Mention classes, activities, paid and unpaid positions that relate. Be specific and strong!

Paragraph 3: Give examples that prove you know how to do the job well. Describe the responsibilities as you know them to prove that you've done your research.

Paragraph 4: State that you are available for an interview and would welcome the opportunity to meet the reader in person. Thank the reader for his or her consideration.

Sincerely,

Your signature

Your name in print

How to Conduct an Interview

Tips on how to prepare for an interview:

- ◆ Research your topic and the person you plan to interview thoroughly.
- ◆ Come prepared with the proper materials (a pen, paper, tablet, and preferably a way to record his or her voice).
- ◆ It is a good idea to have a list of questions already at your fingertips. The best questions are those that you can't answer by Googling. You want the subject to respond in a unique way.
- ◆ Don't assume they have the time or the desire to meet you. Be polite and *ask* if they would give you some time, and give them an approximate length of time that it will take so they can plan accordingly.
- ◆ Arrive dressed for success.
- ◆ Be on time.

Tips on interviewing a subject:

- ◆ Use eye contact.
- ◆ Ask a question that you've prepared, and *listen* to the response. Then ask a question based on the response that you might not have prepared. Show your subject that you are listening.
- ◆ Shake their hand in greeting and when saying good-bye.
- ◆ Say thank you.

Tips on how to wrap up your interview:

- ◆ When the interview is over, go somewhere where you can reflect on everything that you remember. Jot down notes about clothes, wall colors, books on their table, etc. Details will help your final presentation.
- ◆ Write a thank you letter. Make sure it includes a greeting, a reminder of the interview, and a mention of the top few points that were particularly helpful, and end by signing your full name. Remember to use formal, academic language and correct conventions, even if it's in an email!

QRF (Question-Response Format)

Using the correct paragraph structure is really important. If you were building a skyscraper, you wouldn't want the roof stuck in between floors and the basement on top, right? Of course not. There's an order to things that helps support your ideas. When we write expository, factual essays, they are made up of a bunch of QRF paragraphs (Question-Response Format). We use QRF as a standard structure that gets our ideas out in a clear way.

Here is a brief description of a QRF paragraph:

The first sentence is the main topic sentence.

It's beautiful. You can't miss it. It really makes a statement, and it says something about what your paragraph will be about. You might want to take a sentence or two to expand on your main topic.

The next section is the evidence.

This is the proof that your reader needs to believe what you have to say. Your opinion is not enough; you need facts to back up your thoughts. Evidence can be found in quotes from the text, interviews, data, statistics, etc.

The next section is commentary.

Commentary is the original thinking that you add to the evidence. What do you think of it? Does it remind you of anything? Have you ever shared the experience?

The final sentence is the conclusion or transition sentence.

It's like the ground floor of the building. It's where you leave the paragraph behind, walk out onto the street, and into a different topic.

Oral Conference Feedback Sheet

OWN YOUR OWN FEEDBACK!

Ok, so I'm going to sit down with you to give feedback on your essay. During this meeting, you are to take notes to use as a reference later when you are revising or finalizing your paper.

THESIS STATEMENT NOTES:_____

_____

_____

This is great, keep doing it,   To be revised, considered,
don't change a thing!   mulled over, overhauled

Based on the essay in front of me today, my teacher is giving me a (enter grade)
Think about it: Am I satisfied with that? Y / N

Due date of final draft based on our discussion:

Signed: _____   Date: _____

Norms for Video Conferencing

"Netiquette" is the accepted word for behavior online. It is the expected manners everyone should use when they are communicating virtually.

There are rules of netiquette that apply to video conferencing at home or at school just as there are rules in the classroom when you are responding to someone's writing or ideas.

1. Treat others with courtesy and respect.
2. Don't use bad language: using bad language just proves you don't know how to say something well.
3. Don't spread rumors or lies: use the Internet to spread information, not instigation.
4. Collaborate and share your expertise: if you have an answer, step up and share. Learn from each other. It's what the internet is all about.
5. Lurk before you participate: when it comes to video conferencing, listen first to the conversation and know your audience and your setting before choosing your tone or words.
6. Be forgiving: everyone's a newbie at sometime in their life. Everyone misspeaks occasionally or offends someone by accident because they haven't perfected their online voice yet. Let the small things pass, and pick your battles.
7. Don't distract others: if there is a guest online and we are listening to what that person has to say, don't be a distraction in the background.
8. Don't hijack the discussion. Stay on topic.
9. Bring something new to the conversation.
10. Cite your sources with links or other resources. If we are allowing you to backchannel while the guest is speaking, provide resources and links to back up any further information you want to share.

A reminder to those who set up their own accounts; make sure you:

- Protect your profile: when you set up, click on the appropriate box to make sure that your information isn't public.
- Don't conference anonymously: let people know who is calling.
- Ask first, before you call: if you see someone online, send him or her a chat box first with the phrase, "Are you available to video conference?" Don't just call.

Developing a Student-Created Assessment

When you take an assessment, you are proving what you know about a topic. But did you know that developing the assessment itself can also prove what you know about the topic?

To develop an assessment, you need to know the topic, but you also need to know how to ask questions and the types of questions that you can ask. We, the teachers, use a variety of questions to keep students engaged as well as to make sure that different kinds of learners are given the chance to show off what they know.

In the following activity, you will be identifying questions as one of the following: forced choice, rank order, or open-ended. The first one has been done for you:

1. Should the dress code be enforced in school? **Forced choice**
   a. No, it's a silly rule that shouldn't be around anymore.
   b. Yes, if it's a rule, then it should be enforced.

   Why did you select your answer? <u>I selected forced choice because there were only two available options I could choose, and both were selected by the test creator.</u>

2. How should the US deal with persons coming from an Ebola zone if they don't show signs of infection? Mark a 1 for the option that you believe is most likely to help the problem. Mark a 5 for the option that is least likely.
   ___ Quarantine them in a hospital or treatment center regardless of their lack of symptoms.
   ___ Test them at the airport based on where they are traveling from.
   ___ Let them return home and put them under house quarantine for 21 days.
   ___ Let them return to their lives unless a symptom occurs.

   Why did you select your answer? _____

3. What can we do to save electricity at home? _____
   _____
   _____
   _____

   Why did you select your answer? _____
   _____
   _____

4. What statement best describes your attitude toward homework: _____
   a. It's necessary.
   b. It's a waste of time.
   c. It helps me learn, but there's too much!
   d. It helps me learn, but I wish I had more practice.

Why did you select your answer?_____

Now to apply what you've learned: in the activity below, develop three questions based on your topic of choice. Make one question a Level 1 question. Another should be a Level 2 question. The third should be a Level 3 question.

Feel free to use the following keywords to help design your questions:

◆ Level 1: Questions that are Level 1 include sentence stems that ask them to recite, define, describe, list, etc.
◆ Level 2: Questions that are Level 2 include sentence stems that ask them to infer, compare/contrast, sequence, categorize, etc.
◆ Level 3: Questions that are Level 1 included sentence stems that ask them to judge, evaluate, create, hypothesize, predict, etc.

Final reflection: do you notice a correlation between kinds of questions and levels of questions? If so, what?_____

_____

_____

_____

How to Annotate Text

We annotate text in order to help learn its contents. But did you know that how you interact with a text is also a great indicator of how deeply you understand that text?

We talk about annotation as interaction because, in a strange way, it creates a relationship between you and what you are reading.

Below is a step-by-step process of reading and annotating your text. These methods will help you tease apart, figure out, decipher, engage with, question, comment on, disagree with, and explore your documents and books.

- ◆ Step 1: Read the text through once for just overall pleasure and understanding. If you don't understand something, just plow on through and you'll loop back to it in your second reading. (It's also possible that you'll get it in your second reading anyway. Sometimes things are just like that.)
- ◆ Step 2: Read it again with the purpose of annotation.

Possible ways to annotate:

- ◆ Put a ? in the margin next to anything that you think is confusing. Scribble the question beneath it.
- ◆ Put a (★) next to anything you find interesting.
- ◆ Put an ! next to anything you find surprising.
- ◆ Highlight things you believe will prove important. Watch out for this one, however. Remember that highlighting should be used minimally. Not everything is important.
- ◆ Circle any lines that repeat.
- ◆ Put a (☺) next to something that shows a positive bias.
- ◆ Put a (☹) next to something that shows negative bias.
- ◆ Draw a book in the margins if a passage reminds you of something you read before.
- ◆ Draw a globe in the margin if a passage reminds you of something in the news or around the world.
- ◆ Create a symbol that represents you. Draw that doodle in the margin if a passage reminds you of something in your own life.
- ◆ Write a brief summary at the bottom of your document so you can quickly reflect and refer to the gist of the writing.

Remember that annotating text is like having a conversation with it. Sometimes having a conversation is messy and loud. Your paper and your annotations should reflect that.

Visual Presentation (PowerPoint) Guidelines

When people give oral presentations, they always highlight their talk with visuals. Visual presentations help add another layer of information to your material. They also help engage your audience so they are focused on you and your topic for a longer period of time.

There are many different ways and many different programs out there to help you create a visual presentation for your oral presentation. PowerPoint, Prezi, Keynote, or Google Presentations are just a few programs that give students access to high-quality presentation software.

However, to create a great visual presentation, you can't just copy and paste parts of your essay onto a few slides. There are some rules you can follow that will bump up your level of presentation creation.

1. **Avoid huge blocks of text:** paragraphs are for essays, not presentations. Don't put in your presentation what you plan to say. Your audience can read, after all, and it's a waste of time to make a presentation that really is just your script.

2. **Don't use bullets:** or, at least use them sparingly. Presentations are to add visuals, charts, graphs, pictures, etc., not words. The words should come from your mouth, not the slide. The visual on the screen should highlight what's being said, not cue or substitute what's being said.

3. **Always remember you are on stage:** look at your audience. Use great eye contact, and don't be lured in to look at your own presentation.

4. **Practice, practice, practice:** don't have the first time you are in front of the class be the actual first time you have run through your presentation. Make sure you have memorized your material and have practiced enough to know your approximate times. Also, test all technology before your deadline so you can troubleshoot if necessary.

5. **Use the programs to their best advantage:** if there are animation techniques to help your text or images move, why not use them? Don't rely too heavily on this, however. After all, it's meant to engage your audience and act as a visual highlighter. But your presentation should reflect what you know about using the program; for instance, if you are using Prezi, make sure you have an image that captures the main idea of your topic as the "bigger picture" image that is made up of all your own slides along the Prezi path. For Keynote, there are tons of things to play with, but make sure you use them sparingly. Don't explode every slide!

6. **Use tons of different kinds of visuals:** there are so many ways you can highlight your main topic or your evidence. You can display charts, graphs, and data. You can have quotes from polling results fly in. You can insert short videos. The list is endless. Don't be trapped to mere text.

7. **Get feedback before your final presentation:** present in front of family. Present in front of friends. Most importantly, present in front of yourself. Record yourself doing your presentation. Watch it and make note of what you want to improve when you are in front of the class.

Advocacy/Argument Outline

I. Introduction
   a. Hook
   b. Background information
   c. Who is affected by this issue?
   d. Thesis statement
      i. Possible structure: *Opinion + Reason #1 + Reason #2*

II. Body paragraph(s): Reason #1 and Reason #2
   a. Main topic sentence (general statement)
   b. Expands on the main topic sentence (because surely there is more to say on the topic than just one sentence!)
   c. Textual evidence
      i. Quote
      ii. Statistic
      iii. Data
      iv. Personal experience
   d. Commentary/connection to the evidence
      i. Connect to self, media, world, etc.
      ii. Predict
      iii. Relate to a metaphor or simile
      iv. Question
      v. Visualize/describe in detail
      vi. Evaluate/give an opinion
   e. Transition to next paragraph

III. Counterargument
   a. Main topic sentence (states the opposing side's *best* point)
   b. Expands on the point
   c. Textual evidence that includes the strongest case for this side
   d. Commentary/connection
   e. Conclusion that *refutes* this point (i.e., why it's not enough to convince you)

IV. Conclusion
   a. Reiterate thesis (uses different words)
   b. Solution/call to action

Remember to keep the six traits in mind. You can never write without them close at hand: sentence variety, voice, word choice, proper conventions, great ideas, easy to follow organization.

References

"11 Ways to Increase Your IQ Score (Intelligence Quotient)." *Mental Health Daily*. Web. 30 Jul. 2015. <http://mentalhealthdaily.com/2013/04/24/11-ways-to-increase-your-iq-score-intelligence-quotient/>

"21st Century Skills Definitions." *Institute of Museum and Library Services*. Web. 17 Dec. 2014. <www.imls.gov/about/21st_century_skills_list.aspx>

"The 30 Smartest Celebrities In Hollywood." *Yahoo Finance*. Web. 30 Jul. 2015. <http://finance.yahoo.com/news/the-30-smartest-celebrities-in-hollywood-175417855.html>

Andreasen, Nancy C. "Secrets of the Creative Brain." *Atlantic*. Atlantic Media Company, 2014. Web. 30 Jul. 2015. <www.theatlantic.com/features/archive/2014/06/secrets-of-the-creative-brain/372299/>

"Animal Games." *Gamesxl.com*. Web. 30 Jul. 2015. <http://animal.gamesxl.com/>

"Apple Think Different Ad (1997)." *YouTube*. YouTube, n.d. Web. 30 Jul. 2015. <www.youtube.com/watch?v=nmwxdgm89tk>

Barry, Barnett. "Why Is Project Based Learning Important?" Email interview. 28 June 2014.

"BrainPOP—Potential Energy—Movie." *BrainPOP*. Web. 30 Jul. 2015. <www.brainpop.com/science/energy/potentialenergy/preview.weml>

Cloud, John. "Is Genius Born or Can It Be Learned?" *Time*. Time Inc., 2009. Web. 30 Jul. 2015. <http://content.time.com/time/health/article/0,8599,1879593,00.html>

"Conservation Scientist." *Crossing Boundaries*. Web. 30 Jul. 2015.

Cox, Lauren. "5 Experts Answer: Can Your IQ Change?" *LiveScience*. TechMedia Network, Sep. 2012. Web. 30 Jul. 2015. <www.livescience.com/36143-iq-change-time.html>

"Creative Commons." *Creative Commons*. Web. 30 Jul. 2015. <http://creativecommons.org/>

Cruz, Emily. "Theme Park PBL Unit." Email interview. 4 Feb. 2015.

"Debunking Myths about Gifted Students." *Edutopia*. Web. 30 Jul. 2015. <www.edutopia.org/blog/debunking-myths-about-gifted-students-heather-wolpert-gawron>

Dolphin, Warren D. "Writing Lab Reports and Scientific Papers." *McGraw-Hill College Division*. Web. 30 Jul. 2015. <www.mhhe.com/biosci/genbio/maderinquiry/writing.html>

"The Downside of Genius." *Psychology Today*. Web. 30 Jul. 2015. <www.psychologytoday.com/blog/innovation-generation/201307/the-downside-genius>

"Employers' Challenge to Educators: Make School Relevant to Students' Lives." *MindShift*. Web. 30 Jul. 2015. <http://ww2.kqed.org/mindshift/2014/06/23/employers-challenge-to-educators-make-school-relevant-to-students-lives/>

"English Language Arts Standards." *Common Core State Standards Initiative*. Web. 30 Jul. 2015. <www.corestandards.org/ela-literacy/>

"Explore Math with Desmos." *Desmos.com*. Web. 30 Jul. 2015. <http://desmos.com/>

"Facts about Force: Push and Pull." *Easy Science for Kids*. n.p., Jan. 2013. Web. 30 Jul. 2015. <http://easyscienceforkids.com/all-about-force-push-and-pull/>

"Find Curriculum." *Teach Engineering*. Web. 30 Jul. 2015.

Hoenigmann, Eric. "Break-Even Analysis Assignment." Email exchange. 3 Feb. 2015.

"How Geniuses Think." *Creativity Post*. Web. 30 Jul. 2015. <www.creativitypost.com/create/how_geniuses_think>

"The Identification of Students Who Are Gifted." *ERIC Digest*. Web. 30 Jul. 2015. <www.ericdigests. org/2004-2/gifted.html>

"Improving Intelligence." *Psychology Today*. Web. 30 Jul. 2015. <www.psychologytoday.com/ blog/exploring-intelligence/201302/improving-intelligence>

Juliani, Aj. *Inquiry and Innovation in the Classroom: Using 20% Time, Genius Hour, and PBL to Drive Student Success*. London: Taylor & Francis, 2014. Print.

Kyle, Mike. "How Do You Use Project Based Learning?" Email interview. 30 June 2014.

"Mathematics Standards." *Common Core State Standards Initiative*. Web. 30 Jul. 2015.

"Mensa Workout." *Mensa International*. Web. 30 Jul. 2015. <www.mensa.org/workout>

"Multiple Intelligences Self-Assessment." *Edutopia*. Web. 30 Jul. 2015. <www.edutopia.org/ multiple-intelligences-assessment>

"Newton's 3 (Three) Laws of Motion." *YouTube*. YouTube, n.d. Web. 30 Jul. 2015. <www.youtube. com/watch?v=mn34mnndnku&feature=youtu.be>

"Next Generation Science Standards." *Next Generation Science Standards*. Web. 30 Jul. 2015.

"Nicola Tesla." *Wikipedia*. Wikimedia Foundation, n.d. Web. 30 Jul. 2015. <https://en.wikipedia. org/wiki/nikola_tesla>

Orphal, David. "Why Is Project Based Learning Important?" Interview. n.d.: n.p. *Facebook*. Web.

"Punnett Square Calculator." *Science Primer*. Web. 30 Jul. 2015. <http://scienceprimer.com/ punnett-square-calculator>

"Rube Goldberg." *Rube Goldberg*. Web. 30 Jul. 2015.

"StudyJams." *Scholastic*. Web. 30 Jul. 2015. <http://studyjams.scholastic.com/studyjams/ jams/science/forces-and-motion/force-and-motion.htm>

"Switch Zoo Online—Make New Animals." *Switch Zoo*. Web. 30 Jul. 2015. <http://switchzoo. com/zoo.htm>

"Tell-Tale Signs of a Genius Child." *BBC News*. Web. 30 Jul. 2015. <www.bbc.com/news/ uk-england-hampshire-17702465>

"Weebly." *Weebly.com*. Web. 30 Jul. 2015. <http://weebly.com/>

"Welcome to the Purdue OWL." *Purdue OWL: APA Formatting and Style Guide*. Web. 30 Jul. 2015. <https://owl.english.purdue.edu/owl/resource/560/01>

"What Is Human Intelligence?" *Curiosity.com*. Web. 30 Jul. 2015. <https://curiosity.com/playlists/ what-is-human-intelligence-xativnc0/?utm_source=dsc&utm_medium=rdr&utm_ campaign=rdrwork#intro-playlist>

"What Is Quirky?" *Quirky: The Invention Platform*. Web. 30 Jul. 2015. <http://quirky.com/>

"Where Is the Fastest Roller Coaster?" *Wonderopolis.org*. Web. 30 Jul. 2015. <http://wonderopolis. org/wonder/where-is-the-fastest-roller-coaster/>

"Wix." *Wix.com* [free website builder]. Web. 30 Jul. 2015. <http://wix.com/>

Wolpert-Gawron, Heather. *'Tween Crayons and Curfews: Tips for Middle School Teachers*. Larchmont, NY: Eye on Education, 2011. Print.

Wolpert-Gawron, Heather. *Writing Behind Every Door: Teaching Common Core Writing in the Content Areas*. New York, NY: Routledge, 2014. Print.

"You Can Increase Your Intelligence: 5 Ways to Maximize Your Cognitive Potential." *Scientific American Global RSS*. Web. 30 Jul. 2015. <http://blogs.scientificamerican.com/guest-blog/ you-can-increase-your-intelligence-5-ways-to-maximize-your-cognitive-potential/>

Zapato, Lyle. "Pacific Northwest Tree Octopus." *ZPi*. Web. 30 Jul. 2015. <http://zapatopi.net/ treeoctopus/>